THE NORTH IRISH HORSE

D1805926

BATTLE REPORT:
NORTH AFRICA AND ITALY

BELFAST :
W. & G. BAIRD, LTD.
1946.

THE NORTH AFRICAN CAMPAIGN :

21st JANUARY—20th MAY, 1943.

After two months' beet-pulling in the fields of Norfolk the regiment was celebrating Christmas, 1942, when on 27th December news came through that we were to proceed overseas almost immediately. The vehicles were to leave within a few days, and the personnel shortly after that. The Commanding Officer, Lt.-Col. D. Dawnay, was on leave in Ireland at the time and the Second-in-Command, Major The Lord O'Neill, was at the Senior Officers' School. Major J. Rew immediately set to work to prepare the Regiment for abroad, and, due to his excellent organisation and the hard work of all ranks, all tanks and vehicles were ready to leave on their appointed days.

After the departure of the vehicles the Regiment was allowed to proceed on embarkation leave, the average length of which, including travelling time, was six days. A few who had to remain on duty on the boats missed their leave but bore their disappointment well. Shortly before the Regiment left Wickham Market our Hon. Colonel, The Earl of Shaftesbury, K.P., came down to inspect the Regiment and to say farewell He made a most heartening speech which was greatly appreciated by all ranks.

On the night of 20th-21st January, 1943, we steamed out of Wickham Market and arrived next morning at Liverpool where the Regiment immediately embarked in the S.S. " Duchess of York." We cast off from the quayside during the morning of the 22nd January and lay off until 23rd when we sailed to join the convoy. In the early hours of the 24th all ranks were astir to see the Northern coast of Ireland and, as we slowly passed Rathlin Island, Whitepark Bay (where we did our first armoured car T.E.W.T.), Portrush (of happy memories) and Magilligan Point, the men sang with great feeling until the shores of Ireland slowly faded from view.

The voyage was uneventful ; we formed part of a fair-sized convoy with a small aircraft carrier in the centre. As we neared Gibraltar the convoy split in two, one part going round the Cape and seven ships altering course to pass through the Straits. We passed the Rock at 0220 hours on Sunday, 31st January, and many were on deck to see this fine spectacle. There was a bright moon ; the Rock was brilliantly lit and searchlights were sweeping the sky. It was very impressive.

On 31st January we were told that we should arrive next morning and that we might have to march anything up to 17 miles. This prospect was not hailed with delight but nobody believed that it could be true. On 1st February we duly arrived in Algiers, where we were immediately informed that we must disembark forthwith and march 15 miles to our transit camp. The regiment was clear of the boat about 1530 hours and the long march began at 1645 hours. The first few miles were through the cobbled streets of Algiers which did not give our feet a very good start. The regiment, however, stuck it out manfully, and with the aid of whistling and singing we arrived shortly before 2200 hours, to find that our billets consisted of wine vat buildings with stone floors. It certainly was a very long 15 miles.

On 4th February, the regiment, less a composite party consisting chiefly of A Squadron, left Algiers by boat for Phillipville. We had been promised some excitement by the Navy but the voya ge proved uneventful and we duly arrived at Phillipville on the morning of 5th February.

From 5th to 19th February we were busily engaged in unloading our vehicles at Phillipville, Boujie and Algiers. Matters were further complicated by the fact that one ship in the vehicle convoy had been forced to return to England with twenty-two tanks and seventeen 3-ton lorries on board. This ship arrived in Bone in a later convoy on 21st February. On 19th February the regiment left Phillipville for Le Kef by road while our tanks were going forward by transporter and by rail. During the next few days we had tanks and vehicles scattered over a very wide area of North Africa, all on their way to, or waiting to leave for, Le Kef. A large proportion of the regiment reached our harbour near Le Kef on the evening of 20th February.

Early next day news came in that the Germans had made a determined push, had succeeded in forcing the Kasserine Gap and were advancing rapidly on Thala. The 6th Armoured Division was immediately switched to meet this threat, and Brigadier R. H. Maxwell was put in command of the defence of Le Kef. For this he had a small mixed force of tanks from N.I.H. and 51st Battn. Royal Tank Regt., all the tanks available of 142nd R.A.C. with one troop of ours in addition having been sent off to Sbeitla the day before we reached Le Kef. This mixed force of tanks was put under command of Lt.-Col. Timmis, commanding 51st Battn. Royal Tank Regiment and a force consisting of five companies of infantry (two of which were the headquarters personnel of N.I.H. and 142nd Regiment, Royal Armoured Corps), two troops anti-tank guns, a detachment of Royal Engineers, were placed under command of Lt.-Col. Dawnay. In addition, several tanks from 6th Armoured Division workshops in Le Kef were to be used as pillboxes under the command of Major E. V. Strickland. The organisation of this defence went on from 21st to 24th February, during which time Le Kef was dive-bombed three times, very little damage being done. By 24th February the Germans were retiring back again towards the Kasserine Gap and we returned to our harbour outside Le Kef.

On 26th February Lt.-Col. Dawnay was ordered to go to head-quarters, 78th Division, to report to Major-General V. Evelegh, with the object of receiving preliminary instructions for the employment of the N.I.H. in the area Medjez El Bab-Sloughia.

Lt.-Col. Dawnay met Major-General Evelegh as he was leaving his headquarters and was immediately taken out to see a battle which had suddenly developed in the area. The Germans had made an attack at first light and had succeeded in making a considerable advance. The 11th Infantry Brigade, however, threw the enemy back and took a good number of prisoners. As there had been much enemy activity along the whole front Lt.-Col. Dawney, on returning to headquarters 78th Division, took the precaution of having Advanced 5th Corps rung up to find out if there had been any alteration of plan. He was informed that the regiment would not be going under command of the 78th Division immediately but that there were no plans as yet for its employment. Lt.-Col. Dawnay then drove quietly back to the regiment's harbour area near Le Kef where, on arrival, he at once saw that something was on. He was told that he was wanted urgently at headquarters, 25th Army Tank Brigade, and when he arrived there found that orders had already been given to Major Rew, Major The Lord O'Neill still being in Bone marshalling the last boat load of tanks and vehicles.

Our destination was Beja. A strong German attack with tanks had been launched against Sidi Nsir and a very grave threat was developing against our positions at Hunt's Gap. We were to move at top speed all through the night. Lt.-Col. Dawnay issued orders and left for Beja at 1930 hours with his Intelligence Officer, Lt. P. Francis, and A and B squadron Reconnaissance Officers, Captains P. C. M. Sinclair and A. K. E. Finch Noyes. He arrived at Beja at about 0100 hours and went immediately to headquarters 46th Division, where he met Brigadier Maxwell who took him in at once to see Major-General H. A. Freeman-Attwood. Lt.-Col. Dawnay was told that the situation was rather grave, that Sidi Nsir had fallen and that it was essential for our tanks to be in position by first light. He was then given instructions as to the two localities which our tanks were to occupy and was informed that he came under command of Brigadier James, V.C., M.C., commanding 128th Infantry Brigade. Meanwhile the regiment consisting of A Squadron less one troop and B Squadron less two troops, had left harbour at 2000 hours and was proceeding along the winding, hilly road to Souk El Arba. It was a pitch black night and rain was falling heavily. The road surface was treacherous and to make matters worse the route was choked with transport. By 0300 hours it was obvious from reports coming in from the military police that the tanks could not possibly reach Beja by first light.

During the early hours of 27th February Lt.-Col. Dawnay worked out his orders and arranged for his two reconnaissance officers to be taken forward by two divisional liaison officers to do a reconnaissance at first light. He then sent the Brigade L.O. back to bring forward Majors Rew and Ketchell to receive orders at the level crossing at Beja before the arrival of the tanks. Orders were given out to Major Rew and Major Ketchell at about 0630 hours and the tanks, which arrived at approximately 0700 hours, were immediately refuelled. In a very short space of time, despite the fact that the lorries with the petrol had been diverted by the military police and had to be found, the two squadrons were on their way to their localities. By 0900 hours they were both in position.

B squadron on the right occupied a locality to the West of Djebel Munchar and A squadron took up a position in " The Loop " just to the north-east of Ksar Mezouar station. This latter position proved to be the key to the defence of Beja : it blocked the defile which was formed by an anti-task obstacle and mines extending to the south as far as Djebel Munchar and by hilly and mined country to the north. If the enemy had succeeded in forcing a way through this gap, their armour would have debouched into the rolling country to the north-east of Beja and nothing would have saved that town. If Beja had fallen it would probably have meant a withdrawl of the allied line to a distance of over fifty miles.

During the afternoon of 27th February both the squadrons took stock of their positions and liaised with the infantry. A squadron were mortared a little bit and in moving a troop at the infantry request so as to have a Besa shoot, Sjt. Allen's tank was hit in the engine by a shell from an anti-tank gun or tank and was knocked out : another tank was hit on the track, which was broken. There were no casualties. After last light the squadron withdrew to harbour near Sidi Mimech. B squadron harboured in their own locality.

Before first light on 28th February A squadron returned to take up their position in " The Loop " and while doing this Major Ketchell's tank was hit by an anti-tank gun, Sjt. Walters and Tpr. Nursey being instantly killed and Major Ketchell badly wounded. The Squadron 2nd in Command and Reconnaissance officer, Captains R. J. Griffith and P.C.M. Sinclair, were not present owing to broken-down tanks and the command of the squadron devolved for the time being upon Lieut. W. R. Hern. It was not long before reports began to come in to Lt.-Col. Dawnay, whose Headquarters was situated at Headquarters, the 128th Infantry Brigade, at Sidi Mimech, of enemy armour manœuvring in the area. Orders were immediately given to Captain Sinclair that on no account were his tanks to go forward to engage the enemy but he was to wait for them to come on to him. Major Rew was then ordered to leave one troop in his locality by the Munchar and to lead the remainder of his squadron to take up a position around Ksar Mezouar Station. This was successfully accomplished without loss and Major Rew took over local command of the area comprising " The Loop," Ksar Mezouar Farm, " T " Road west of Djebel Munchar and Ksar Mezouar Station, Capt. Griffith, who arrived at about 1100 hours, being in command of A squadron in " The Loop." Major Rew immediately made a reconnaissance, liaised with the infantry and organised his defensive positions quickly and effectively. After mid-day enemy activity increased and their armour continued to manœuvre around probing for a

6

weak spot. About this time Lieut. Hern had a shot at a Mark VI and holed it through the turret. At the same time he was hit by a ricochet and wounded in the back of the neck. He was immediately evacuated. At 1400 hours the enemy put in his real attack and advanced along the more easterly road of the " Antlers " with the object of forcing his way through the defile. This attack was met by our tanks, the anti-tank guns in the area and heavy artillery fire and was decisively defeated, several enemy tanks being set on fire and knocked out. Shortly after this Capt. Griffith proceeded to headquarters, 2nd/4th Hampshires, and on his return reported a number of German tanks in the valley out of range of our 6-pounders. The location of these tanks was given to the medium artillery who put down a concentration for about 30 minutes and, when darkness fell, Capt. Evans, R.E., went forward and found one disabled German tank which he blew up.

In the evening of this day the German armour formed up again with the obvious intention of putting in another attack. Our reconnaissance troop, commanded by 2nd Lieut. H. E. Irwin, which had done invaluable work in providing extra observation posts throughout the day reported this concentration of tanks and the medium artillery was immediately brought to bear on this splendid target with disastrous results to the enemy who, after one tank had been hit, were thrown into a state of confusion. Next morning their tanks were found abandoned.

During the night of 28th February—1st March, the German infantry put in an attack and shortly after first light succeeded in driving our infantry off the high feature, Point 374, immediately to the north of " The Loop." This meant that we were completely overlooked from the north and gave the enemy the most perfect observation posts. Our infantry at that time was not sufficiently strong to put in an immediate counter-attack and commander of the 46th Division made application for the use of the corps reserve which consisted of only one infantry battalion, the 8th Argyll and Sutherland Highlanders.

On the morning of 1st March, Capt. Griffith went forward on foot and entered one of the six German tanks which had been abandoned the previous evening. He brought back a wallet and other equipment which was immediately sent to Headquarters, 128th Brigade Major Rew then made a plan to blow up these tanks. Brigadier James heard of this but decided that there would not be sufficient explosive available on the spot and he ordered Capt. Evans to go forward with a party of R.E.s to destroy these tanks. While Capt. Evans was collecting this party it was decided to put down a heavy concentration of fire on to the area of the abandoned tanks and Lt.-Col. Dawnay gave orders over the wireless that nobody was to go forward until Capt. Evans arrived. There was a misunderstanding over this and when the artillery fire came down it was found that Capt. Griffith was in the area and the fire had to be hastily called off. Immediately Capt. Griffith returned this fire was again put down. Meantime Capt. Evans left in a 15-cwt. truck full of explosive and he reached Ksar Mezouar safely. Almost immediately after the explosive had been removed from the truck enemy aircraft appeared and scored a direct hit on the vehicle. The R.E.s then proceeded to make a reconnaissance and towards the end of an eventful afternoon, which had seemed a very long one to those waiting anxiously at Sidi Mimech, all the enemy tanks were successfully destroyed. .

Throughout the day the Germans put down intense mortar fire at intervals and just before last light more armour was seen manœuvring in the valley. The artillery again open up on this area and dispersed the enemy tanks.

During the morning of this day C squadron reached Beja and Major Welch was immediately sent forward to make a reconnaissance of " The Loop " with the idea of relieving A and B squadrons that night. In the afternoon, however, we received orders that three troops were to be despatched immediately to Sedjenane. Major Welch was thereupon ordered to leave with his reconnaissance officer in a scout car and three troops and to move on tracks through the night.

On 2nd March the remaining two troops of B squadron and regimental headquarters troop arrived at Beja. The two B squadron troops were immediately sent forward to Major Rew and the R.H.Q. Troop was left in reserve at Beja where it was heavily dive-bombed during the day but suffered no casualties. Early in the day a report came in that another German Mark VI tank was in the area of those previously destroyed and that this was bogged aṅd abandoned. It was hoped to effect recovery but later in the day the R.E.s had to go forward and blow it up.

Enemy armour and infantry began in the morning to manœuvre in the area round El Guessa Farm, which had fallen during the night of 1st-2nd March, and prepared to make an attack on Montagne Farm. This eventually materialised during the afternoon and our tank crews at Ksar Mezouar Station saw this attack go in. Enemy infantry were seen advancing. For a moment our men thought that the farm was lost. Suddenly it was observed that the enemy were not advancing to the attack but were in the act of surrendering. It was a moment of great relief. Shortly afterwards these prisoners were on their way to Sidi Mimech where they stated that the artillery fire had been more severe than that experienced in Russia and that they could stand no more.

During the night of 2nd-3rd March the 8th Argyll and Sutherland Highlanders arrived in the area to relieve 2nd/4th Hamps, the commander, 46th Division having obtained permission to use the Argylls to restore the positions captured by the German infantry on the night of 28th February-1st March. At 1000 hours on 3rd March this attack was put in. The two companies on the left were successful but the company on the right was unable to reach its objective owing to intensive mortaring and machine-gun fire. During the afternoon Lt.-Col. Dawnay received orders from the divisional commander that he was to send one troop to advance north as far as a small house by d'A Haneeb, along the winding road which led behind the newly-captured enemy position at Point 374.

The object of this was to keep the enemy's heads down by fire while the Argyll Company, which had failed in the morning, advanced again on its objective. It was known that the road was mined and that there was a small enemy anti-tank gun guarding the road. No. 2 Troop A Squadron, commanded by Lieut. J. A. Ballantyne, was selected for the task and the following plan was made :—

1700—1705 hours—Concentration on anti-tank gun.

1702 hours—Smoke from close support tank on enemy minefield and anti-tank gun.

1703 hours—Party of R.E.s advance in carrier to lift mines.

1705 hours—Smoke from artillery to shield right flank of troop advance to start line.

Four Brens from Reconnaissance Troop in position to cover lifting of mines.

1706 hours—Troop to advance to start line.

Troop to advance from start line when signal, which was carefully arranged, was given by R.E.'s who had also an officer in the leading tank.

R.E.s to re-board carrier and same operation to be repeated if further minefields met.

The concentration and smoke were put down according to plan and the enemy reacted immediately with very accurate machine-gun and mortar fire. The carrier conveying the sappers was hit and ditched, one sapper being wounded and the remainder going to ground. The troop leader called for more smoke from Capt. Griffith in the close support tank and then ordered the troop to advance although no signal had been received from the R.E.s. On the point tank reaching the minefield the R.E. officer advised that they should not go on but the troop leader decided to continue with the advance. The point tank was blown up and the other mines exploded in sympathy. The troop leader's and the reserve tank passed through but the latter was hit several times by mortar shells and broke a track. Lieut. Ballantyne, showing great determination, continued and reached his objective from which he reported that none of our infantry was in sight. The Argyll company failed to take the objective. The troop leader was then ordered to return after which nothing further was heard on the wireless. The tank was seen next day lying abandoned and from inspection at a later date it was obvious that it had been mined as it was returning. Lieut. Ballantyne and two of the crew have since been reported as prisoners of war in Italy. The crews of the other two tanks remained in their tanks until after midnight when, having decided that it was impossible to effect recovery that night, Lt.-Col. Dawnay gave the order to immobilise and evacuate. The crews carried out this operation successfully and arrived back in " The Loop " at about 0200 hours.

On the morning of 4th March A and B squadrons, who were still in position in " The Loop " and Ksar Mezouar Station, were heavily mortared. Major Rew, while looking out of his tank, was killed by the blast of a mortar bomb. His death was an irreparable loss to the Regiment ; his organisation of the defences of Hunt's Gap in most difficult conditions was splendidly executed. Capt. G. P. Russell immediately took over command of the squadron. On 5th March Major E. V. Strickland, who had been commanding Brigade H.Q. squadron, arrived to take over A squadron.

Meanwhile C squadron had reached Tamara at 0400 hours on 2nd March and a report by Major Welch on the action which took place on that day is now included :—

At 1900 hours, 1st March, three troops C squadron were ordered to support the 139th Brigade at Sedjenane. They arrived at Tamara at 0400 hours Tuesday morning. I had made a reconnaissance with the officer commanding Lincolnshires the night before, being under his command. His orders were to hold Sedjenane as a firm base. The enemy had infiltrated through the positions of the Forresters, 1st Commandos and the Durham Light Infantry and had driven them from their positions during Monday's fighting. The Colonel of the Lincolns asked me to dominate Sedjenane at first light and to support his infantry. I moved two troops to the village and one troop on to the Mansour Ridge to watch the left flank. All were in position by 0900 hours. The troop dominating on the right of the road was in a bad position due to difficult ground and the Germans managed to infiltrate right up to this troop. On the whole, however, the day was quiet and the Germans were held. At dusk the squadron was ordered to withdraw to harbour. The right-hand troop when retiring got caught by the dark owing to pulling out a carrier. As a result two tanks, after taking a wrong turning, went over a small cliff by a mine pit shaft.

At 0200 hours Wednesday, 1st Commandos began to retire and reported that the Lincolns were still in Sedjenane and that they were surrounded. The Brigadier ordered the tanks to advance at first light and to drive the enemy from the village. No infantry or artillery support was possible. The tanks advanced down the road and encountered no opposition until the outskirts of the village where the point tank was knocked out by a shot from a 50 mm. anti-tank gun, which penetrated the front plate and started an ammunition fire. The crew, except for one, were killed or wounded by snipers. The tanks then shot up the village and the Germans retired except for snipers. I tried to get infantry support into the village but could only get one platoon. The Germans, as soon as they realised that there were no infantry with us, started to infiltrate back and to snipe. Our infantry were unable to cope with this. My tanks remained in their positions without support until I made contact with O.C. Lincolns, who had received orders to retire. He arranged to meet me again at 1600 hours.

During all this time heavy mortar and artillery fire was put down on the tanks, with several casualties, including the forward observation officer. At 1500 hours the Adjutant of the Lincolns came up and said that they were going to retire and asked me to cover their retirement. I advanced to the outskirts of the village and told the tanks there to open fire to assist the infantry, ordering one troop to the Mansour Ridge to cover my withdrawal. The fire put up by the tanks in the village was good and a lot of Germans were killed. Our infantry came out on our right through the woods and moved down the road. I smoked the village and hill on the right during this operation. I remained in observation for half-an-hour and saw nothing ; I then moved back to the Mansour Ridge, sending the troop there one bound further back.

Just as it was getting dark we came back through the Coldstream Guards who had come up to form a firm base, the majority of 139th Brigade and 1st Commandos being safely back. Numerous petrol and ammunition dumps were destroyed by our tanks as we returned and we also pulled out a 6-pounder gun which had been left behind. One tank of No. 1 troop, in trying to pull out some other guns, was bogged and had to be destroyed.

On 6th March the Commander of the 46th Division ordered an operation to take place which consisted of a drive from the road Beja-Djebel Abiod by one parachute battalion to clear any enemy from the high ground north of Sidi Mimech and an advance by one company of 2nd/4th Hamps supported by one troop N.I.H. from Chemical Corner to Zouave Corner. No. 2 Troop B squadron, commanded by Lieut. J. H. Pyl, was selected for the task and Lieut. Pyl received orders at headquarters 46th Division at 1700 hours. At 2400 hours the troop moved off from Sidi Mimech and arrived at 0230 hours, 7th March, at Chemical Corner after a difficult march along a bad road on a dark and rainy night. At 0300 hours the Hamps company arrived and the plan was made. The force moved off at 0600 hours along the road towards Zouave Corner, the paratroops moving through the hills on the southern flank, and by 1100 hours had reached a point west of Farm La Forestiere. No. 2 Troop now only consisted of two tanks, one having broken down earlier in the morning. The infantry fanned out and advanced on the farm supported by the tanks and by 1200 hours the farm was in our hands without a shot being fired. The infantry immediately started to dig in and the tanks gave flank protection. At 1230 hours heavy mortar and machine-gun fire suddenly rained down on the farm and the infantry withdrew, suffering casualties. No. 2 Troop covered the withdrawal and endeavoured to locate the enemy. Lieut. Pyl's tank was hit several times by anti-tank rifle fire and it was soon evident that the enemy fire was coming from positions to the north. Lieut. Pyl then made three journeys in his tank, collecting the Hamps' company commander and some wounded and carrying them to a rallying point, while his troop serjeant remained on the objective covering this operation.

During the afternoon Lieut. Pyl and Sjt. McAughtry took forward two officers and two other ranks in their tanks and put them back in the farm. The tanks then took up hull down positions. Soon after this more heavy fire came down and the position was finally evacuated at 1700 hours. The force then withdrew and arrived back at Chemical Corner at 1900 hours. On their way back Sjt. McAughtry's tank broke a track and a guard was provided for the night by the R.E.s. A splendid feat of quick repair was accomplished and the troop returned to the regiment on the morning of 8th March.

On the evening of 7th March, Tactical Reconnaissance reported that the enemy armour was withdrawing north-east and this was confirmed next day. During these operations liaison with the artillery was excellent. Lt.-Col. Graham acted as local C.R.A. to Brigadier James and had a seat in his L.C.V. Information from his own observation posts, our tanks and the infantry, kept pouring in on all wirelesses and results were very satisfactory.

The activities of C squadron now form the main interest and Major Welch at this time was under command of 1st Parachute Brigade. Many small actions were fought.

On 8th March about 1200 hours, one troop of C squadron under Lieut. J. E. Williams, with Capt. Sidebottom in support in a close support tank moved up the road Djebel Abiod-Sedjenane to support 1st Parachute Brigade in driving out the enemy who had infiltrated into our positions in the area round Sidi Moh Belkassen. The four tanks supported the paratroops into the south-west corner of the wood east of the road. The paratroops cleared both sides of the road and drove the enemy into the north east corner of the wood on Rag Bou Krachiba. The paratroops now asked Capt. Sidebottom if he would take his force forward to a position east of the road Sejenane-Djebel Abiod. To this Capt. Sidebottom agreed and got his force into a good position in the open ground. The paratroops bolted the enemy from the area and the tanks got a good shoot at enemy infantry in the open. The number of enemy killed could not be ascertained but they were thrown into considerable confusion and 157 prisoners were taken, including five officers. The co-operation between infantry and tanks was excellent.

On 9th March the corps commander ordered a reconnaissance in force and himself detailed the force to consist of two platoons of infantry and six tanks. The tank force was subsequently reduced to one troop with a close support tank in support At 1415 hours the force advanced with infantry on the right and tanks, completely road-bound, on the left. The point tank went over an unlocated minefield safely but the troop leader, Lieut. J. E. Williams, had his tank blown up. The reserve tank got past after lifting mines but was too late to support the point tank which was found on fire approximately 600 yards away. Major Welch, in the close support tank, supported the infantry into a wood on the right, but after a short time the infantry commander decided to retire and this was covered from the close support tank with smoke. The reserve tank then withdrew and picked up Lieut. Williams and crew en route. Approximately 27 prisoners were taken and some useful information was obtained. Throughout the day the road was under very heavy mortar and artillery fire.

During the period 10th-16th March one troop was maintained with the Parachute Brigade, and this task was carried out alternately by No. 2 and No. 5 troops. They took part in small engagements daily and had many unpleasant nights in the forward area. On 11th March, 2/Lt. R. E. Perioli's troop supported 1st Parachute Battalion with Besa fire in the area about Ahmed Baleus from 1100—1200 hours, when an attack was made eastwards : the tanks supported from the right flank. A number of enemy infantry was seen but the results of the fire could not be checked. At 1400 hours Capt. R. D. Morton in a close support tank, together with Lieut. J. E. Williams' troop supported 2nd Parachute Battalion with Besa fire from the high ground north of Rag Bou Krachiba. No enemy were seen then but when 2nd Parachute Battalion later succeeded in advancing on to this ground some 100 enemy dead were found. On 12th and 13th March one troop remained in an anti-tank role covering the Sejenane road and a further troop took up a position on 12th March to cover the area about Djebel Abiod. This latter troop was withdrawn at first light on 13th March. Whilst engaged in these operations the squadron harboured in an area near a mine on the road Beja-Djebel Abiod.

On 14th March we nearly lost our Padre, Capt. E. M. Hughes, who was on his way to take a service with C squadron. He was attacked by an enemy aircraft which shot up his car most accurately and caused him and his driver great discomfort in a nearby ditch for several minutes. The Padre got a lift on to the harbour, took his service there and returned in time to conduct a Memorial Service in the B squadron lines for Major Rew. Every man in the regiment was thankful for his escape.

In the Beja sector from 8th March until 6th April the regiment, less three troops of C squadron, remained in the area Hunt's Gap-Beja and during this time troops occupied a position round Ksar Mezouar Farm and, on several occasions, Sidi Ameur, by day and night. On the night of 20th-21st March two troops of A squadron, under command of Capt. Griffith, had to move back into " The Loop " position owing to a reported threat of enemy armour from the area. " The Loop " was occupied by them all the following day and they had a most unpleasant time, being most accurately mortared and shelled by the enemy who had observation posts on the high ground immediately to the north.

The 128th Infantry Brigade was also ordered at this time to provide a counter-attack force which consisted of infantry, tanks, anti-tank guns and artillery, and was placed under command of Major The Lord O'Neill. The infantry for this force was found successively by 2nd-4th Hamps, 8th Argyll and Sutherland Highlanders and 1st Royal Irish Fusiliers, who occupied the stop line which ran, from 16th March onwards, north and south astride the road Beja-Ksar Mezour about two miles to the east of Sidi Mimech.

By 17th March the German pressure had increased along the northern front and it was decided to withdraw to a line running roughly north-west to south-east through Djebel Abiod, which was definitely to be the stop line. The 139th Brigade arrived about this time to reinforce 1st Parachute Brigade and the Sherwood Forresters took over from 3rd Parachute Battalion in the area round Tamara. No. 5 troop C squadron, which was at Tamara, was withdrawn on the evening of 17th March before it got too dark and it was as well that this step was taken, since during the night 17th-18th March the Forresters withdrew.

On 18th March No. 2 troop C squadron helped to cover the withdrawal of 139th Brigade and 2nd Parachute Battalion back to the Djebel Abiod line. Major Welch moved his harbour that day to a position along the road Tabarka-Djebel Abiod. On 20th March, No. 2 troop, commanded by 2nd Lt. Perioli, took part in a moonlight attack on Nefza Station in support of one company 2nd Parachute Battalion. It was very difficult to see but 2nd Lieut. Perioli successfully joined his infantry and gave them all possible help into the station which the Leicestershires had reported as being occupied by the enemy. On arrival no Germans were found on the position, but a strong patrol was driven off down the railway line.

On 27th March the 46th Division offensive began. The C squadron troops were under command of 138th Brigade and had to make a very difficult night march on 27th-28th to a rendezvous south-east of Djebel Abiod to join up with the Lincolns by 0600 hours on 28th March. This was not helped by the fact that the R.Es. were late in clearing a minefield outside Djebel Abiod, but the rendezvous was reached on time. At 0600 hours on 27th March personnel of the Lincolns mounted the tanks and the advance began towards the mine above Sedjenane. This force at once came under fire from the feature immediately to its front, despite the fact that it had been reported clear. The Lincolns continued to advance and were supported by our tanks until a wadi was reached which was found to be uncrossable. The tanks accordingly stopped in position there and covered the York and Lancs and King's Own Yorkshire Light Infantry who also had to advance up the hill. At least two enemy machine-gun posts were put out of action and five prisoners were taken as a result of our supporting fire. During 29th and 30th March the C squadron force remained in reserve at the ford in this area and on 31st March moved up the road Djebel Abiod-Sedjenane with 8th Argyll and Sutherland Highlanders. This was very slow work due to mines and very heavy enemy aircraft attacks. Lieut. J. E. Williams' tank got a direct hit from an aircraft but none of the crew was injured and the tank was safely evacuated. Meanwhile No. 2 troop was supporting the 8th Argyll and Sutherland Highlanders who were held up in the woods west of Sedjenane, and No. 5 troop under Lieut. Whelan was trying to get up the track to the mine to help 6th Royal West Kents, but was stopped by darkness. At about 1200 hours Brigadier Howlett was put in command of this

14

sector by Commander, 5th Corps, Lieut.-General C. W. Allfrey, who ordered Sedjenane to be taken that night. This was successfully accomplished.

On 1st April, 2nd Lieut. Perioli arrived before the bridge to the west of Sedjenane and found it blown. With the help of the R.Es. he managed to cross the ford and to advance through Sedjenane into an area which was very heavily mined. Lieut. Whelan continued his advance towards the mine, which was occupied by the Lincolns just before he got there. There was again very heavy air attack all that day. That evening No. 2 troop lost one tank on a mine and was compelled to remain in Sedjenane for the night. On 2nd April, 138th Brigade took over from 36th Brigade who pushed forward and found that the Germans had gone right back and that to the north 1st Parachute Brigade was advancing with the object of clearing Cape Serrat with the aid of the Goums. These French toops did magnificent work throughout the campaign. On 3rd April all C squadron troops were allowed to withdraw into harbour and from then until 12th April remained in reserve in a big wood to the west of Sedjenane. On 12th April, with the exception of one troop which was left under command of 2nd U.S. Corps which had relieved the British in the northern sector, this C squadron force returned to Beja. On 13th April C squadron, less one troop, which was now under command of 12th Brigade, was ordered out to Ksar Mezouar but was not used and was withdrawn next day.

On 2nd April, Lt.-Col. Dawnay was summoned to attend a Conference at headquarters, 46th Division. He was surprised to meet there Major-General Evelegh, commanding 78th Division, and his brigadiers and C.R.A. Major-General Evelegh then gave out that there was to be an offensive which was to start on the night 6th-7th April and which embraced the capture of Djebel Dourat, Djebel Outiah, Point 512 and Point 624 on the right, and Djebel En Nahel, Mergueb, Chaouach and Point 667 on the left. The regiment was to come under command of 36th Infantry Brigade, commander Brigadier B. Howlett, D.S.O., for these operations. After much reconnaissance and an explanation of the plan on a cloth model at headquarters 78th Division, we had a quiet day on 6th April in readiness for our night march. The following report on the operations was submitted to Brigadier R. H. Maxwell, Commanding 25th Tank Brigade, by Lt.-Col. Dawnay :

During the night 6th-7th April, N.I.H., less C squadron H.Q. and four troops, moved from Beja to Oued Zarga heights. We started to move forward again at 0330 hours and the artillery opened with a tremendous roar at 0350 hours. Passing through Oued Zarga we got into position due south of Point 226 near Sidi Ameur Ben Rhibi

The 5th Buffs meantime had attacked Djebel En Nahel before first light and had succeeded in capturing this feature except for an obstinately held little pimple on the northern slopes. Two troops, one B squadron and one C squadron, under Capt. Finch Noyes, were immediately sent to co-operate and

15

shortly afterwards Brigadier Howlett instructed me to send the remainder of B squadron.   Capt. Finch Noyes then worked round the right flank and the enemy fled from the pimple, abandoning two infantry guns, while Major Russell took three troops of his squadron to Point 259 and on towards the Oued Bouneb which he successfully shot up and from which the enemy withdrew.   During this movement two tanks ran on to a minefield and were damaged.

The next phase of the operations as far as 36th Brigade was concerned was the capture of Mergueb Chaouach.   The plan was for the Argylls to work up the Oued Bouneb and 6th Royal West Kents to use Oued Maiou.   A and B squadrons were to cross the Oued Bouneb near Italian Farm and then support the infantry forward over the open and up the slopes on to the objective.   The start was fixed for 1600 hours but the infantry were late due to mines and difficult going in the oueds and the operation did not begin until shortly after 1730 hours.   Owing to the infantry being late B squadron was forced to stay in the open near Point 226 awaiting 6th Royal West Kents while A squadron managed to remain concealed near the Oued Bouneb.

The advance was a complete success and, although casualties were suffered by the infantry, Chaouach was in our hands by 1900 hours.   Towards the end of the advance our squadrons were dive-bombed but Spitfires appeared out of the clouds and shot down eight Stukas, the pilot of one landing by parachute near Major Russell's tank.   Owing to the delay the artillery were forced to keep their programme going for nearly two hours.

N.I.H. then returned to harbour in the assembly positions of the morning.

On 8th April the 5th Buffs were ordered to secure Point 667 which is the highest feature in the vicinity   A squadron was ordered to support by moving on the Buffs' left flank as far up the slopes as possible.   When the Buffs reached Oued El Djeb they were held up by fairly strong opposition and suffered some casualties.   A squadron moved up to this wadi to help them to advance, and was then heavily shelled by our own artillery. The Buffs continued the advance and two troops of " A " squadron under Capt. Mackean crossed the oued by a defile after he had removed enemy mines.   These two troops then turned east and took up a position near a white house on the slopes up to Point 667, which soon after was captured by the Buffs.

Enemy tanks were reported in the valley at 1030 hours and they manœuvred there for the remainder of the day.   Heavy concentrations of medium artillery were brought to bear on them and they immediately changed position.   It is thought that they were acting in a delaying role and hoped that our tanks would go forward towards them.

I ordered up B squadron during the middle of the day and they occupied hull down positions on the south side of Oued El Djeb.   During the day we were subjected to three dive-bombing and machine-gunning attacks and had a lot of Besa shooting. Before last light the two troops of A squadron were successfully withdrawn after experiencing anti-tank and high explosive fire on the way back. A squadron harboured on the western slopes of Mergueb Chaouach, and Regimental Headquarters and B squadron went further back to their original assembly position.

At 0730 hours on 9th April the enemy counter-attacked the Buffs on Point 667 and at 0800 hours two troops A squadron under Lieut. Hern went forward to support our infantry from an area near the white house. Enemy tanks were again seen in they valley and artillery fire was brought on to them. At midday I went forward to make a reconnaissance and sent Major Strickland up towards his two troops near the white house to make another reconnaissance. As a result of my reconnaissance I ordered B squadron through the defile to take up hull down positions on the far side. Shortly after 1500 hours B squadron, from their new positions, saw an abandoned enemy 85 mm. gun and, after looking carefully for booby traps, managed to tow it in.

At 1530 hours the enemy again counter-attacked Point 667 but were beaten off by the Buffs. Shortly after 1700 hours Major Strickland returned with information that there were eight Mark VI German tanks in beautiful hull down positions in the valley with other Mark IV's and Mark III's put forward as a bait.

I decided to have a go at these tanks and arranged for artillery fire to be brought down on them while the two troops on the high ground manœuvred to have a quick shoot from a favourable ridge. This was done twice by the two troops and although observation was very difficult one hit on a Mark VI was claimed. Subsequently the regiment withdrew and harboured on the western slopes of Chaouach.

Throughout the day our positions were subjected to frequent dive-bombing and machine-gunning attacks from the air.

On 10th April after sending for all available tanks from Beja and conferring throughout the night I arrived back at the harbour at 0400 hours and immediately issued orders for the regiment to move out at 0530 hours. By first light A and B squadrons were in position east of the white house on the slopes of Point 667.

The plan was as follows: The 38th Irish Brigade, supported by one troop C squadron, was to advance from Djebel Mahdi and seize Djebel Oum Guerinat and N.I.H., less C squadron, was to engage any enemy tanks found in the valley. To carry out the latter part of this plan I moved with A and B squadrons to the position given above and left a force under command of Major The Lord O'Neill consisting of spare tanks, two troops anti-tank, one section 17-pounders, and one section R.Es. to form a firm base on the northern side of the defile which crosses the Oued El Djeb.

17

At 0700 hours I took Major Strickland forward on a personal reconnaissance on foot and could see no movement in the valley except for a small party of Germans. On moving further forward we could see into the Doctor Bed Valley and we noticed a lot of transport moving north east. This seemed to indicate that the enemy were withdrawing and shortly afterwards I ordered A squadron to advance north towards Point 361. This was done very cautiously with one troop in front and the feature was reported clear with no signs of the enemy in the valley. I immediately ordered B squadron to move north west and to occupy Point 391.

Realising that I could help the attack of 38th Brigade if I could reach Djebel Rmel I wirelessed this proposal to my liaison officer with 38th Brigade and received an answer that this move would be very helpful. Consequently I ordered the advance to continue on a two squadron front towards Djebel Rmel. Shortly afterwards A squadron was held up on a minefield and made slow progress but B squadron was able to move quickly up to some high ground to the west of Djebel Rmel. I followed the B squadron centre line and quickly directed them on to Djebel Rmel itself which was occupied after engaging retiring enemy infantry with Besa fire. Meantime A squadron had successfully negotiated the minefield and moved to a position south east of the Farm Der Rmel. While repairing the track of his tank which had been broken by a mine, Lieut Gardiner was wounded but managed to complete his task before he was evacuated.

Orders were then received that our positions were to be held and that infantry would be sent to relieve us before last light. During the afternoon efforts were made to bring up self-propelled guns and 17-pounders to engage two enemy tanks which were standing broadside on in a farm to the east of Rmel but the self-propelled guns got ditched and the 17-pounders could not be found A great chance was thus missed.

Persistent air attacks also took place and during the course of one of these an Me.110 was shot down by Besa fire and crashed in flames. Subsequently the 30 mm. cannon was rescued from this aircraft.

At about 1700 hours the enemy brought forward an anti-tank gun into a Wog hut at the northern end of the Rmel. In dealing with this B squadron had one tank in Lieut. Brown's troop penetrated by a 50 mm. shell and the forward gunner was killed. The anti-tank gun was knocked out by Major Russell's 3 in. Howitzer and several prisoners were taken. On the right A squadron worked forward but could not get into position to engage the two enemy tanks which were to their front.

At last light there was no sign of the Black Watch who were to relieve us and they did not take over our positions until approximately midnight. I determined to hold the positions at all cost and resorted to firing Besa at intervals at likely approaches, and putting up one or two parachute flares. No attack by the enemy was made. Both squadrons spent the night in small laagers to the rear of their day positions.

The attack of the 38th Brigade was completely successful and very little opposition was encountered. Many enemy were seen to leave the El Guerinat and nearby features when we occupied Rmel. The C squadron troop, commanded by 2nd Lieut. Mann, supported this advance very well but did not get very much shooting.

Both A and B squadrons remained out in the area Djebel Rmel until mid-day on 11th April, when it was decided to withdraw except for one troop of A and one troop of B ; these subsequently returned to harbour at last light. We were now under command of 4th Division.

The 12th April was a quiet day for the tanks until the afternoon, when a message was received that the Black Watch, in trying to change over a forward company which had been heavily shelled, with a rear company, had taken the forward company off before putting the rear company on, with the result that enemy fire prevented the re-occupation of the forward locality. Two troops of tanks were sent out to support the infantry but were not used and a platoon making a counter-attack after dark failed to re-establish the position which had been occupied by the enemy after last light.

Owing to the failure of the Black Watch to re-establish the forward locality I was sent for during the night 12th-13th April and with the Gunner made a plan for a composite squadron of A and B squadrons, under the command of Major Russell, to support the Black Watch on to the forward objective. This was achieved soon after first light. During the course of this day 2nd Hamps went forward on to Djebel El Guerinat which had not been re-occupied after 38th Brigade had been pulled out. This advance was not contested by the enemy.

During the morning Capt. Leslie, our E.M.E. and Lieut. Ball, Technical Adjutant, arrived at Oued Zarga to supervise repair work at the new workshop which had just been set up there. They had only been there a few minutes when enemy aircraft attacked and Capt. Leslie was killed and Lieut. Ball wounded. This was a very severe loss to the regiment and necessitated the appointment of Lieut. Garner, who was Recovery Officer, as E.M.E. and Lieut. Wilson, who was commanding R.H.Q. Troop, as Technical Adjutant.

In the afternoon a plan to put a company of the Black Watch on to the 350 feature was abandoned as it was felt that it was wiser to leave this bare feature unoccupied and to include it in the defensive fire tasks. The tanks, however, remained in the area until last light when they withdrew to harbour near the Oued Bouneb.

On 14th April the regiment moved to a harbour just to the south of Oued Zarga where it was joined by No. 5 troop C squadron, and where we prepared for the last phase of the campaign. We soon heard to our intense satisfaction that we were to come under command of 78th Division who at this time were having some very hard fighting. This resulted in the capture of the Chaouach and Toukabeur but not of Tangoucha or Heïdous, each of which proved the scene of violent attack and counter-attack.

On 19th April, Major-General Evelegh unfolded the plan to the brigadiers and Lt.-Col. Dawnay. The next day it was explained in greater detail to company and equivalent commanders on a cloth model and the Army Commander spoke to the assembled officers. The regiment had the good fortune once again to come under command of 36th Infantry Brigade, which was given the important role of the capture of Longstop. By 1200 hours, 22nd April, reconnaissance and conferences had been completed and we were ready for the tasks ahead.

The following report of the battle for Longstop is based on the report submitted by Commander 36th Infantry Brigade to 78th Division :—

The battle of Longstop started at 2245 hours, 22nd April, when the 6th Royal West Kents and 5th Buffs left their start line to the east and west of Chassart Teffaha. Their objectives were : 6th R.W.K.—Chaibine and the ridge to the north ; 5th Buffs— Djebel Bechtab, Point 196 and Point 303. 8th Argyll and Sutherland Highlanders were in reserve ready to pass through the forward battalions on to Longstop, with the object of securing Djebel Rhar before daybreak. 1st Surreys, from 11th Infantry Brigade, under command 36th Infantry Brigade for this battle, with N.I.H. in support, were prepared to exploit along the road east of Longstop. N.I.H. left their harbour at Oued Zarga at 1930 hours and proceeded along the road Medjez-Oued Zarga. All went well until near Medjez 2nd Lieut. Perioli's tank went up on a deeply laid mine over which many tanks had already passed. Fortunately the track did not break although six bogies were shattered and the tank was able to move to the side of the road. After this the regiment could only move very slowly and owing to mines had to alter the route to Chassart Teffaha. The speed of advance gradually got slower and slower and stops became more frequent while mines and vehicles of 1st Reconnaissance Regiment, which blocked the road, were being removed. It was only with very great difficulty that N.I.H. reached their assembly area by first light. Everybody, however, was very much heartened by the tremendous artillery fire during the early hours of the morning.

By 0530 hours, 23rd April, 5th Buffs reached their objectives but heavy machine-gun fire prevented 6th R.W.K. from going beyond Chaibine, making it impossible for 8th Argyll and Sutherland Highlanders to carry out their original plan before dawn. It was not until 0800 hours that 6th R.W.K. were able to reach both objectives after B and C squadrons N.I.H. had been sent forward to occupy the Chaibine, where they dealt with machine-gun nests and were then accurately shelled and mortared. Early on 23rd April the brigadier, with Lt.-Cols. Thomas and Dawnay, went forward to make a new plan which was for 8th A. & S.H. followed by 1st Surreys with N.I.H. in support to assault Djebel Ahmera, the western feature of Long-stop. At 1330 hours after heavy artillery concentration the assault started. The 8th A. & S.H. went up the hill with great dash through heavy machine-gun fire. Casualties were heavy, including the commanding officer, Lt.-Col. McNab, the I.O., Capt. Erskine, and the Adjutant, Lieut. McLeish, killed. By 1530 hours after going in with the bayonet, the Argylls captured the hill. Meanwhile, " A " squadron N.I.H. worked round towards Point 196 destroying en route a machine-gun which had held up 1st Surreys. One tank of 5th Troop crossed the wadi and contacted 5th Buffs, eventually reaching a spot from which the commander dominated the valley and Point 196, and from where, despite heavy shell fire, he managed to shoot up certain positions indicated by the Buffs.

B and C squadrons supported the attack from the right flank near Chaibine. By the evening Djebel Ahmera was held by the 8th A. & S.H. and 1st Surreys, both battalions being very much under strength, and by 6th R.W.K., who had moved forward in support, the whole force being under the command of Lt.-Col. Wilberforce, D.S.O., 1st Surreys. In order to protect the right flank and the road running South of Chaibine, a com-posite force composed largely of H.Q. Company personnel from 1st Surreys and 6th R.W.K., a section of Brigade Defence Platoon and anti-tank guns from 256th Battery, under command of Capt. Stewart, 6th R.W.K., took up a position on ridge south of Chaibine. This force remained in position until the brigade was relieved by 11th Infantry Brigade. During the night an attempt by 6th R.W.K. to capture Djebel Rhar failed owing to heavy mortar fire on the forming up point.

On the morning of 24th April a composite squadron N.I.H., with R.H.Q troop to help with covering fire, was assembled on the southern slopes of Longstop to support the infantry. They remained there to take part at mid-day in an operation by 1st Surreys to clear Mosque Ridge and by 6th R.W.K. to capture Djebel Rhar, the eastern feature of Longstop. Intense mortar and machine-gun fire was put down on the infantry as soon as they attempted to advance, the fire from Djebel Rhar being such that it was impossible for 6th R.W.K. to advance. A very small party of 1st Surreys and R.Es. was able to reach the ridge after it had been cleared by the tanks, one of which was damaged by a mine outside the main minefield running down to the road. This tank was successfully evacuated by Capt. Griffith under machine-gun fire. Another tank was brought up, personal weapons were got out and the crew very cleverly transferred to the supporting tank. Just before dark the tanks withdrew from the ridge, the damaged one being protected by infantry patrols. During the morning a warning was received from an intercept that the enemy might counter-attack Point 196 held by a company of 5th Buffs. This attack did not materialise but two troops of tanks were sent to support the Buffs in case of trouble. Throughout the night 24th-25th April two troops remained on the southern slopes of Djebel Ahmera.

During 25th April the Boche had shown signs of withdrawing in front of 38th Infantry Brigade on our left, so it was considered possible that Djebel Rhar might be abandoned during the night. A reconnaissance patrol sent out by 6th R.W.K. to confirm whether this was so was soon very forcibly shown by machine-gun fire that the Boche was still in occupation of the position.

The plan for the capture of Djebel Rhar, which was based on most accurate information obtained by reconnaissance patrols from 6th R.W.K. during the night, consisted of a diversion round the right flank from Mosque Ridge by C squadron N.I.H. and a strong fighting patrol from 8th A. & S.H. followed by the main assault by 5th Buffs supported by N.I.H. less C squadron from the left flank. The brigadier went forward to fight the battle from Lt.-Col. Dawnay's tank.

The attack started at 0830 hours on 26th April, the Boche bringing down the usual heavy mortar fire which delayed the advance of the Argyll patrol, but the C squadron tanks pushed on to the ridge north-east of Mosque Ridge from which the forward observation officer had very good shooting throughout the day. Later the Argylls worked their way forward and cleaned up a number of snipers in the gulleys, capturing about a dozen prisoners. This diversion was most successful as it had the effect of pushing the Boche into the arms of the main attacking force on the other flank and also prevented any withdrawal to the north-east.

On the left the 5th Buffs formed up near Point 196 at 0830 hours with B squadron N.I.H. in front. Boche shelling began before 5th Buffs started to advance, but soon after 0900 hours the battalion moved forward with A company on the right, D company on the left, B company in reserve, and B squadron N.I.H. in support. The infantry advanced along the upper slopes, with the tanks pursuing a parallel course on the lower slopes of Djebel Ahmera. As the advance progressed two troops of tanks worked forward. No. 4 troop on the right silenced a machine-gun post in a re-entrant and then, after Lieut. Brownfield Pope had transferred to another tank owing to his own breaking a track, went on to engage two machine-gun posts, which surrendered. Immediately the Buffs appeared on the north-west slopes of Longstop the battalion was heavily and accurately shelled by infantry, self-propelled and medium guns. At times whole platoons were hidden by bursting shells but they pressed on with magnificent spirit as though taking part in peace-time maneouvres. A machine-gun post then threatened to hold up the advance but immediate action by No. 4 troop silenced it and Sjt. O'Hare, climbing high on the southern side of Point 289, dealt with three more such posts. Major Russell, commanding B squadron, then ordered No. 4 troop to proceed round to the west of the Rhar to find a way up. At the head of the saddle between the Ahmera and Rhar, Lieut. Pope encountered another machine-gun and mortar post and, finally, a 75 mm. gun badly sited to fire down the western re-entrant ; after one round of 6-pounder H.E. and a burst of Besa the crew surrendered. Sjt. O'Hare then tackled the ascent and on reaching the summit after a magnificent climb took over 50 prisoners. Lieut. Pope meantime was working round the western side of the Rhar. Sjt. O'Hare then moved on down the northern slope, shepherding the prisoners along with him.

The forward companies of the Buffs now moved on to their objectives and B company moved up in support of A company. As they moved on to Point 243 and the feature to the left of it, A and D companies received the surrender of an embarrassing number of prisoners, including the C.O. of 111-754 Grenadier Regiment and his four company commanders. On the left, Major Russell aided by Lieut. Pyl and Lieut. Brown, each of whose troops were now reduced to a single tank, moved on to a spur to cover the northern side of the Rhar plain from Rhar to Sidi Ahmed, thus preventing the Boche withdrawing. It is very unlikely that any of the Longstop garrison escaped. Whilst re-grouping on the spur, the squadron was accurately shelled by a heavy gun but No. 2 troop leader spotted the flashes and was able to get the artillery on to it. Unfortunately the F.O.O. was killed whilst directing his guns. The Buffs consolidated on Djebel Rhar, adapting the existing Boche defences and blasting new positions with " Beehives." Whilst the Buffs were consolidating, A squadron 56th Reconnaissance Regiment moved up the road from Chassart Teffaha towards the forward position of C squadron N.I.H. where the squadron commander was able to indicate to the Reconnaissance Squadron some enemy still holding out. These were rounded up, four being killed and about 30 captured. On Longstop over 300 prisoners were taken at a cost to the Buffs of 40 casualties. Throughout the operations from 22nd to 26th April detachments of sappers from 256th Field Company did excellent work with the infantry, tanks and reconnaissance squadron, lifting mines and supervising the blowing of positions with " Beehives." Very fine work was done by 217th Field Ambulance evacuating casualties, and the speed with which this was carried out was greatly accelerated by the use of a proportion of carriers from each battalion.

The final operations, resulting in the capture of Djebel Rhar, were an example of perfect co-operation between all arms, particularly between tanks and infantry. Targets were successfully indicated to the tanks by means of verey lights fired at machine-gun posts, and in one case a 75 mm. gun was dealt with in this manner. The method by which the tanks moved in echelon along the hillside with those higher up moving ahead of those in the valley enabled anti-tank guns to be engaged before they were able to fire on the tanks in the valley.

It is impossible to speak too highly of the support given by N.I.H. or of the steady advance of the Buffs under heavy shell-fire, two factors which made the capture of Djebel Rhar possible.

In the prisoner of war cage the German battalion commander who was responsible for the defence of Longstop, on being questioned about his defences made the following statement : " The Djebel Rhar is one of the strongest defensive positions that one could ever hope to occupy. I would have been prepared to hold it against a full scale British infantry brigade attack. When it was apparent that tanks were being used over the high ground I knew that all was over." Another German officer is reported to have stated : " When information was first received that tanks were being used on the high ground at Longstop it was not believed by the officers." Report on action by 1st troop A squadron, under Capt. R. H. Bowring, during period 23rd-26th April is given as an Appendix to this section.

After three quiet days, commander 78th Division was ordered to push forward along the valley towards Tebourba. C squadron N.I.H. supported this advance and the following action took place :

At 1000 hours, 30th April, C squadron N.I.H. led the 8th Argyll and Sutherland Highlanders on to Points 160, 177 and 202, which necessitated the crossing of two difficult oueds.

By 1115 hours the tanks were on Point 160 and Point 177 and the pre-arranged signal was given to the A. & S. H. to advance. During their advance the infantry met with some machine-gun fire from the gulleys in the high ground north of Points 177 and 202 but succeeded in getting on to these two features.

At 1145 hours three Mark IV German tanks appeared from the direction of Sidi Zekri. These tanks were engaged and hits were seen on two of them. All three tanks then withdrew to the wadi.

At about 1215 hours a Mark IV, equipped with a long barrelled 75 mm. gun, appeared round the right-hand side of Point 177, knocked out Sjt. Elliott's tank, killing the gunner, Cpl. Dickson, and holed Lieut. Mann's tank. Sjt. Elliott's crew baled out and went to ground but 2nd Lieut. Mann's crew stayed put and the co-driver, Trooper Eastwood, drove the tank back out of action but unfortunately overturned it in the bad oued at the bottom of the hill. It was then found that Lieut. Mann and Trooper Whalley were dead.

Just after this another Mark IV appeared over the rise and was hit on the cupola by Major Welch's 2-pounder. It immediately went backwards down the hill and at least one man baled out. No more tanks were seen during the afternoon but heavy shell fire was put down by a big gun which blew a track off Sjt. Johansen's tank. When ordered to withdraw, Cpl. Bone picked up Sjt. Johansen's crew and withdrew first. Major Welch then withdrew the other two tanks to a position south of Sidi Ahmed at 1900 hours and returned to harbour. The infantry had withdrawn about an hour previously.

Sjt. Elliott reported in at about 2400 hours, having waited until it was dark and then made his way down to the A. & S. H. position. In the early hours of 1st May Troopers Rooke and Chapman, the latter wounded, also got back.

During this action it is estimated that ten enemy were killed, fifty prisoners were taken, and several hits were scored on three enemy tanks.

From 1st May it was obvious from various troop movements that 18th Army Group was regrouping. Rumours were circulating freely as to the composition of the break through force and the direction of the attack. We first of all thought that we were to assist in the break through to Tunis but, after order and counter order, to our extreme disappointment, we were finally split into three parts, R.H.Q., and A squadron coming under command of 78th Division, B squadron under command of 1st Division and C squadron under command of 142nd Regiment, Royal Armoured Corps who were to support the 4th Indian Division in the big attack.

The regiment moved to its new harbour areas on the night of 4th May after handing over seven tanks to 145th Regiment, Royal Armoured Corps.

5th May was taken up with reconnaissance by B and C squadrons and final preparation for the big attack by C squadron. In the evening, at 1700 hours 1st Division, with a squadron of 142nd R.A.C. in support, finally occupied the Djebel Bou.

At 0430 hours on 6th May the big attack started. The 4th British Division was on the right and 4th Indian Division, supported by 142nd R.A.C., with N.I.H. C squadron vice their A squadron, and 145th R.A.C., were on the left. 145th R.A.C., supported 5th Indian Brigade and 142nd R.A.C. the 7th Indian Brigade. C squadron N.I.H. passed through the Gab Gab Gap and moved forward to an assembly area. By 0600 hours the first phase of the attack had proved successful and 142nd R.A.C. pushed through the Gap at about 0800 hours. C squadron N.I.H., whose role was to protect the left flank, formed up behind Souissi but the advance was slightly delayed by the infantry, who were late. By 1000 hours 7th Indian Infantry Brigade were on their first objective and immediately afterwards they pushed right on to Aoud Zriga. During this action C squadron captured six 88 mm. anti-tank guns, two of whose crews did not fire a shot.

As C squadron reached the final objective the leading elements of 7th Armoured Division were starting to pass through the hole which had been punched. At the same time 6th Armoured were streaming through on the right. The timing of the whole operation was extraordinarily good and the work of the artillery against enemy anti-tank guns extremely effective and splendidly executed. Only five enemy tanks were seen and they were engaged as they moved away from the final objective which was immediately converted into a firm base by our infantry and anti-tank guns. By 1500 hours C squadron was on its way back to harbour.

On 7th May C squadron joined B squadron under command 1st Division and in the afternoon advanced to put the King's Shropshire Light Infantry into El Bathan without loss. Lt.-Col. Dawnay arrived to take command of this operation but had to return again to 78th Division that night. At 1900 hours C squadron was ordered by commander 3rd Infantry Brigade to carry a company of the Forresters to an area near Djedeida. This was done and C squadron then formed close laager at 0200 hours on 8th May.

On 8th May Lt.-Col. Dawnay was ordered to meet commander 78th Division at Mornaghia at 0600 hours to receive orders con-concerning the entry into Tunis, which had been entered by the leading elements of the armoured divisions the previous evening. A squadron moved off at first light and was routed via El Bathan. Lt.-Col. Dawnay at Mornaghia received orders that a squadron of 142nd R.A.C. was to come under his command and that one squadron of tanks was to go under command of 11th Infantry Brigade and one squadron under command of 38th Infantry Brigade.

During the morning all resistance ceased in Tunis and British troops began to pour into the town. A squadron N.I.H. arrived in the afternoon and Lt.-Col. Dawnay then received instructions to send this sqadron through the centre of the town to an area near Carthage. A squadron, therefore, had the luck to have a triumphal drive through Tunis. The enthusiasm of the crowds knew no bounds and they received a truly magnificent reception.

Meanwhile Major Welch was early astir at 0430 hours to make a reconnaissance of Djedeida. Brigadier Moore, commanding 2nd Infantry Brigade, decided to attack at 1000 hours and ordered C squadron to support the infantry across the river. Major Welch supported this attack very successfully, his own tank having the special task of dealing with a pillbox which was knocked out by 6-pounder A.P. followed by H.E. A very effective smoke screen was put down by the close support tank. Our infantry got across very quickly and took about fifty prisoners.

Major Welch then reconnoitred for a crossing and found a rather deep ford. Capt. Thomas and No. 1 Troop got cross immediately and the remainder of the squadron was put over in a short time. The squadron then deployed and worked round and through buildings and woods in the vicinity. Immediately the tanks appeared about 200 more prisoners were rounded up. No. 4 troop then carried a platoon of the Gordon Highlanders through Sidi Abdullah and No. 3 troop took another to Chuart, both of these places being quickly occupied. Meanwhile Capt. Thomas and another troop were rounding up more prisoners in the corn fields.

Shortly after this B squadron arrived and both squadrons went into harbour in Chuart.

On 9th May after harbouring the night near headquarters 78th Division which was just north-east of Mornaghia, Lt.-Col. Dawnay was informed that there was to be no movement that day for his H.Q. and A squadron. B and C squadrons were still under command 1st Division and remained in the vicinity of Djedeida During the afternoon the squadron of 142nd R.A.C.

was ordered to return to its regiment which was still under command of 4th Indian Division.

On 10th May the regiment received orders to concentrate in an area near Ain El Askar. A squadron had to make the return march through Tunis and received another ovation on their way back. Before midnight the regiment was safely in harbour.

During these last two days the 6th Armoured Division, who had been directed south east towards Hammamet, had carried out a brilliantly executed action against Hammam Lif, which was defended by many anti-tank guns and considered impregnable by the Germans. The 6th Armoured Division then continued on its way to Hammamet. Meanwhile 1st Armoured Division, having worked its way across the hills, arrived at Grombalia and the 4th Division made a circuit of the Cape Bon Peninsula. To the north the 7th Armoured Division moved north to meet the Americans who had captured Bizerta. During these days there were literally hordes of prisoners choking every road. Many units surrendered complete with all their equipment and were allowed to drive their lorries to the nearest prisoners' cage where they made their own cooking and sanitary arrangements. At one particular cage a German band arrived complete with instruments and in a very short time was regaling captors and captives alike with classical music.

After a quiet morning, on 11th May we were informed that Generals Alexander and Anderson were going to take no chances whatsoever with the opposition that remained. General Von Arnim with his personal staff had surrendered, but had stated that he now had no control over his troops who had been ordered by the Fuhrer to fire to the last round and then surrender. Orders were consequently received that the regiment was to come under command of 1st Division, which was to move to an area near Creteville. This movement took place throughout the night 11th-12th May, and the regiment reached their new harbour before first light on 12th May. During this day tanks were not required and the country around was combed by 4th Indian Division, 3rd Brigade and 128th Brigade which had come under command of 1st Division. Lt.-Col. Dawnay with the assistance of the Reconnaissance and Inter-Communication Troops, helped to marshal many thousands of prisoners and to despatch them with escorts to the various cages that were being hastily prepared.

On the evening of 12th May the regiment was ordered to put one squadron under command of 128th Brigade for a final round up of the enemy in the area south east of Djebel Ressas. A squadron was detailed for this job and moved out at first light on 13th May. No opposition was encountered and A squadron were back in harbour again by the afternoon.

The operation on the 13th May proved to be our last in the campaign and the regiment moved to an olive grove just to the west of Hammam Lif on 14th May.

25th Tank Brigade arrived very shortly afterwards and for the first time since leaving England the Brigade found itself concentrated. After two days of intensive maintenance, rest was the order of the day until news of the Victory Parade reached us. At very short notice 30 tanks were made spotless, a regimental flag was produced and the party left for Tunis.

The Victory Parade on 20th May was a great success. Opposite the dais, which was flanked by two Churchill tanks, was formed up a squadron of Churchills in serried ranks. The route was lined by Churchills, Shermans and guns, and Guards of Honour of the Grenadier Guards, the Americans and the French were drawn up. General Eisenhower, General Giraud, General Alexander, General Anderson, Admiral Cunningham and Air Chief Marshal Tedder took the salute.

First came the French, preceded by a large band which played very martial music. They were splendidly received by the crowd and it was grand to hear the magnificent reception which the Goums were given by the British spectators—a fitting reward for their many daring exploits during the Campaign. There followed the Americans who had sent a few picked men from Bizerta, and then came the British contingent, headed by Commander 5th Corps, Lieut.-General C. W. Allfrey, D.S.O., M.C. The British troops looked very proud as they marched by the saluting base to the music of drum and fife and bagpipe bands. The wheeled and tracked vehicles and the guns came right at the end of the procession and were magnificently turned out. A fly-past by the R.A.F. half way through the proceedings was very well executed and most thrilling to watch.

Thus ended the North African Campaign in which our Churchill tanks played a notable part both in defence and attack. Their effect on the morale of the enemy and the way they raised the morale of our own infantry was truly remarkable. Their feats of climbing and fire power proved most disheartening to the enemy. The Churchill tank made its name in no uncertain fashion.

The North Irish Horse came through the campaign with flying colours. The regiment helped to stop a most determined attack on Beja and Djebel Abiod, took part in the very successful operations from Oued Zarga which culminated in the capture of Point 667, the highest peak in North Africa, and the Djebel Rmel ; played a magnificent part in the capture of Longstop and, with C squadron, helped to support 4th Indian Division in the final break through to Tunis. Considering the severity of the fighting, casualties both in personnel and tanks were remarkably light. The regiment fought as a team and the spirit of all ranks was admirable. The Commander of 5th Corps, Lieut.-General C. W. Allfrey, D.S.O., M.C., could not have paid greater tribute to the regiment when he said to Lt.-Col. Dawnay : " Your Regiment has done extra-ordinarily well ; every formation which you have served speaks well of you. I consider that a great compliment."

APPENDIX A.

Report by Capt. R. H. Bowring on the action of No. 1 troop A Squadron, which was detached from the Regiment on 23rd April and came under command of 38th Irish Brigade.

On the morning of 23rd April, soon after arriving at Chassart Teffaha, No. 1 troop A squadron was ordered to move to Kelbine where it would come under command of 38th Irish Brigade. As this troop only had two tanks Serjeant Graham's tank from No. 5 Troop was added to it. No. 1 Troop moved by steep and winding tracks and *en route* had some difficulty in crossing a wadi. After some excellent work by the R.Es. this was safely accomplished. Capt. Bowring then reported to Brigadier Russell and was immediately taken up on to the height of Bettiour to see the enemy positions. As a result of this reconnaissance, Brigadier Russell decided that the tanks could reach Heidous and they were sent up to the head of the valley. As soon as they showed themselves they were accurately shelled by a light gun and withdrew after Serjeant Graham's tank had suffered a direct hit.

On 24th April the troop remained in harbour behind Bettiour. The officer commanding Royal Irish Fusiliers that day sent in a report that there was possible tank country along the Kef El Tiour. Brigadier Russell then planned an attack to take place the next day at 1000 hours to capture Buller's Hill; the troop was also to shoot the enemy out of the rocky face of the Djebel Tangoucha so as to enable the Royal Inniskilling Fusiliers to advance on the other side.

During the night of 24th-25th April the enemy withdrew from Heidous. The attack went in according to plan ; both objectives were captured and approximately 150 prisoners were taken. In the course of this assault an enemy anti-tank gun was met near Heidous but the crew had all been killed by our shell fire. The troop remained in a counter-attack role until last light and then returned to harbour.

No. 1 Troop rejoined A squadron at Chassart Teffaha on 27th April.

ITALY:

APRIL, 1944—MAY, 1945.

From the end of the Tunisian Campaign until late March, 1944, the North Irish Horse remained in North Africa and were located 25 miles west of Bone on the main Phillipville Road. All types of training were carried out during this period and in October, 1943, the Regiment had been warned that they would be required to take part in an operation. Everything was prepared but unfortunately the project fell through.

Earl in January, 1944, Lieut.-Colonel D. Dawnay, D.S.O., was posted as Second-in-Command of 23rd Armoured Brigade. Thus was ended his period of command of the regiment from November, 1941, during which he had trained the regiment in England, commanded it in North Africa and won the respect and thanks of all ranks. His departure was a great loss to the regiment. Lady Katherine Dawnay most kindly agreed to continue as the controller of the N.I.H. Next-of-Kin Scheme.

Major The Lord O'Neill, who had been Second-in-Command, was promoted to the rank of Lieut.-Colonel and assumed command of the regiment as successor to Colonel Dawnay.

In February, 1944, the Commanding Officer visited Italy and learned that, owing to various difficulties, it was unlikely that the regiment would be brought over to the Italian theatre until May. Arrangements were made for all ranks of the regiment to have leave in Tunis during the month of March. This leave was perhaps the most enjoyed of all those taken in North Africa.

On March 26th orders were received for the regiment to be prepared for embarkation to Italy. At this time fighting squadrons were organised on the basis of five Churchill troops. It was now made known that on arrival in Italy two Churchill troops per squadron would be changed into Sherman troops.

The advance party left on April 7th and the main body on April 16th ; half the regiment embarked at Bone and half at Algiers. By the end of April all the tanks had been disembarked and by 5th May the regiment was fully concentrated at Lucera, near Foggia airfield.

Early in May the Commanding Officer went into hospital in Naples and Lieut.-Colonel E. V. Strickland, M.M., who had been Second-in-Command of the regiment after Lord O'Neill had assumed command, came over from the 145th Regiment, Royal Armoured Corps, to assume command.

The regiment carried out exercises with the 2nd Canadian Infantry Brigade from 5th May until 12th May. Orders were received for the regiment to concentrate at Mignano and by 18th May this was completed.

On the night 18th-19th May nothing eventful occurred but all ranks were kept awake by the artillery firing tasks throughout the night from positions in and around brigade headquarters. Learning from the experience of the 2nd Canadian Infantry Brigade, all ranks dug slit trenches automatically from this day onwards. During the night Major R. Johnston, Royal Devon Yeomanry, joined the regiment, and his two forward observation Sherman tanks were retained at regimental headquarters. This regiment was the self-propelled (105 mm. Priests) regiment in support of the 25th Army Tank Brigade.

At 0700 hours, 19th May, the regiment moved, with the entire 2nd Canadian Infantry Brigade group, to a new area approximately four miles south east of Pontecorvo. It was reported that the French had started an assault on Monte Leuca, west of the town, but that all their attempts to cross the Liri river in an effort to get behind Pontecorvo and so turn the Hitler Line, had met with no success.

The 1st Canadian Infantry Division with supporting arms was held up on the enemy outposts of the Hitler Line and some two thousand yards from the road Pontecorvo-Aquino ; the 3rd Brigade was on the right ; 1st Brigade on the left ; and 2nd Brigade with N.I.H. in reserve. 2nd Brigade group had not been committed in any form and was completely fresh, and was to be kept in that state for the assault on the enemy line. 13th Corps on the right of the Forme d'Aquino had not had much success against Aquino itself and according to the poor lateral information it was thought at that time that the right flank of the 1st Canadian Division was exposed. Monte Cairo, east of Highway 6, was still in enemy hands so that all activities of Canadian Corps were open to view by the enemy. In the Liri valley, behind Canadian Corps, was situated all the 13th Corps and Canadian Corps artillery, augmented by an Army Group R.A. It was clear that the main defences of the Adolf Hitler Line were based on the road running east to west between Aquino and Pontecorvo. This road was some five miles in length and all approaches to it were difficult, the country being densely wooded, with occasional clearings. Existing tracks were very poor and one-way only. At this time all intelligence reports indicated that the line was not fully manned by the enemy.

In the evening the commanding officer explained the situation to squadron leaders but was unable to give out any orders. Major P. Welch, M.C., acting as second-in-command, arrived at approximately 1700 hours with Major A. W. A. Llewellen-Palmer, D.S.O., M.C., who had been appointed second-in-command, but the commanding officer ordered Major Welch to continue as second-in-command for the battle.

On the 22nd May it was reported that fifty enemy tanks had been seen arriving near Pontecorvo from the west. They were engaged by artillery and the " Cab Rank " (fighter aircraft) and five were claimed as knocked out. The remainder dispersed.

At 2100 hours the regiment started the move to the forward assembly area which was some 600 yards short of the start line.

31

Major R. J. Griffith, M.C., who had previously done a reconnaissance of the forward assembly area and start line, led the regiment with A squadron ; B and C squadrons followed, then regimental headquarters, and the regimental aid post vehicles and, despite some mortaring and " nebelling," the regiment collected in the forward assembly area by 2330 hours without casualties. The regimental aid post was to be amalgamated with the Infantry regimental aid post by " H " hour and light scale echelon supplies were to be brought up under Major Welch's arrangements to the forward assembly area. Between 2330 hours, 22nd May, and 0400 hours, 23rd May, A, B, and C squadrons linked up with their infantry and the normal regimental link was included with the Tactical Headquarters, 2nd Canadian Brigade, which was situated approximately one thousand yards south east of the start line. Air photographs of the line were issued down to reconnaissance captains.

The 23rd May, 1944, was the day of the Adolf Hitler Line battle. There had been plan and counter-plan ; order and counter-order going on since 18th May, but, finally, the Army Commander visited 1st Canadian Division on 22nd May and the following general plan was formulated :

The 1st Canadian Division would assault the Hitler Line with two brigades of infantry, each supported by a regiment of Churchill tanks and preceded by a block barrage from approximately 600 guns. The division would assault on approximately a three thousand yards front ; 2nd Brigade with N.I.H. on the right ; 3rd Brigade with the 51st Royal Tank Regiment (R Tks.) on the left, and the first objective would be the centre part of the Pontecorvo-Aquino road.

Brigadier Gibson's plan was to attack two battalions up : Princess Patricia's Canadian Light Infantry with A squadron N.I.H. in support on the right ; the Seaforths of Canada with B squadron on the left ; C squadron was to support B squadron. The Loyal Edmonton Regiment, supported by B squadron 51st R. Tanks was to follow up and pass through the Princess Pat's once the first objective had been consolidated. " H " Hour was 0600 hours.

The commanding officer allotted a forward observation officer from the Royal Devon Yeomanry to each of A and B squadrons. The Reconnaissance Troop, under Lieut. H. E. Irwin, M.C., was to remain under regimental control.

THE ATTACK

At " H " minus 15 hours artillery opened up on located enemy mortar and gun positions and the barrage commenced at " H " hour. Infantry and tanks linked up successfully on the start line and the attack went in to time. However, it appears that the movement of N.I.H. to the forward assembly area and forming up point, and the artillery barrage, had warned the enemy of the direction of our attack for immediately our advance started the enemy brought down heavy concentrations of artillery and mortar fire about 100 to 200 yards behind our barrage, as a result of which casualties were inflicted on the infantry. The enemy made good use of air bursts just behind the barrage, where he expected to find our infantry. The first five hundred yards of the attack from start line were through dense country in which were situated several enemy strong points and in the trees were found snipers many of whom had strapped themselves to the trees. Dust caused by the barrage cut down visibility to approximately ten yards. By 0730 hours the tanks reached the edge of the woods and were faced by open ground leading to the fringe of trees and scrub on the objective. The distance to the objective was not more than four hundred yards from this point, but by this time all communication between tanks and infantry on the No. 38 set failed owing to infantry casualties amongst No. 38 set personnel.

A squadron, with some of the Princess Pat's, found that they were held up by a cleverly concealed minefield and were engaged with fire from various types of anti-tank guns. In this confused fighting this squadron lost two tanks on mines and four to enemy anti-tank weapons but in their turn destroyed one Panther Mark V, two Mark IVs. and two 75 mm. anti-tank guns as well as several snipers and enemy infantry posts. It is interesting to note here that this was the first Panther tank knocked out by the Allies in the west. Major Griffith controlled most of this operation, which lasted some six hours, on foot and under heavy fire. He ordered Lieut. D. F. Hunt to try and find a way round the right of the minefield but this officer was able to report that the right was blocked by deep wadis into one of which his Churchill turned a complete somersault.

At 0800 hours Major G. P. Russell, M.C., led the move of B squadron out of the wood and across the open ground towards the objective. One hundred yards from the objective very heavy anti-tank gun fire was opened on this squadron as a result of which five tanks, including those of Major Russell and Capt. M. B. Pope, M.C., were knocked out. Major Russell was seriously wounded, Capt. Pope slightly. Major Russell's tank was found later to be not more than thirty yards from a Panther turret emplacement but tank commanders could not see more than ten yards at this time owing to the dust. Lieut. J. H. Pyl, however, on the left of B squadron, reached the objective with his troop and there found some of the Seaforths who pointed out a house to him which was two hundred yards beyond the objective and from which they said they were being heavily engaged. Lieut. Pyl's troop immediately destroyed this house and silenced all opposition from it, after which operation he withdrew his troop to join the remaining tanks of B squadron. Capt. W. M. Mackean, M.C., now commanding B squadron, advanced into the clearing, but was immediately engaged by enemy anti-tank guns. Under cover of smoke he succeeded in extricating his tank from this position, but the tank was then knocked out by another enemy anti-tank gun. Captain Mackean and his crew evacuated the tank but were pinned to the ground by enemy machine-gun fire.

At approximately 1200 hours the commanding officer was informed by 25th Army Tank Brigade that enemy tanks were known to be in the area between 2nd and 3rd Brigades so he moved the regimental headquarters' tanks, including the self-propelled battery commander's Sherman, to the left flank.

Brigadier Gibson informed the commanding officer at approximately 1300 hours that the remnants of the leading companies of the Seaforths had succeeded in reaching the first objective but that they were being attacked by enemy tanks and had only Piats with which to defend themselves. The commanding officer formed a composite force of the remaining tanks of B and C squadrons and put them under command of Capt. C. M. Thomas. Fortunately this officer was in possession of a mosaic aerial photograph and by using this the commanding officer was able to guide Captain Thomas and his force away from, and around, the clearing which was now known to be the enemy tank killing ground. This force reached the objective but was unable to find any trace of the Seaforths. At this juncture, this force came under very heavy enemy artillery fire, three tanks being hit almost immediately and knocked out by heavy calibre shells, probably 210 mm. Captain Thomas displayed great coolness and judgment and ordered the force to disperse slightly. At this point the commanding officer ordered Captain Thomas to withdraw to a position from which he could dominate the objective but, unfortunately, in trying to carry out this order the force came under heavy fire from many enemy anti-tank guns as a result of which seven tanks were destroyed, including Captain Thomas's. Lieut. G. Mahon's troop of three tanks, before being themselves knocked out, destroyed an enemy Panther turret emplacement and a 75 mm. anti-tank gun. It is interesting to note that both the Churchill 6-pounder and Sherman 75 mm. easily penetrated the Panther turret and that the Besa not only penetrated the two shields of the 75 mm. anti-tank gun but also killed the crew. The range was two hundred yards.

Captain Thomas and the survivors were heavily engaged by enemy machine-gun fire when they evacuated their burning tanks.

At this stage Major Griffith reported the presence of several enemy tanks and self-propelled guns on the west bank of the Forme d'Aquino and near the road. After a reconnaissance he decided not to use artillery against them owing to the presence in that area of men of the Princess Pat's, but asked for Sappers to gap the minefield in front of his squadron. The Sappers, despite casualties, did gap the minefield in one place and two Churchills led by Sjt. Best advanced through the gap only to be knocked out on the far side by cleverly-concealed anti-tank guns.

The Adolf Hitler Line had now been overrun twice by tanks, and men of both the Princess Pat's and Seaforths had reached the objective. It is true that both infantry and tanks sustained heavy casualties in doing this but enemy resistance began to slacken at approximately 1600 hours and it was at this stage that the Pontecorvo wing of the enemy line folded up. Major Griffith was ordered to form a firm base in his area with Princess Pat's and the

Loyal Edmontons, and Brigadier Gibson ordered up anti-tank guns. The commanding officer ordered the remnants of B and C squadrons to rally near the start line and by using the regimental headquarters tanks less the Commanding Officer's, another composite force was formed here under Captain Mackean who had returned on foot.

There was still considerable enemy activity in and around the Forme d'Aquino and A squadron, under Major Griffith, were fired at by machine-guns throughout the night.

Unfortunately just before last light on this day a chance Nebelwerfer burst landed in the regimental headquarters and C squadron refuelling area as a result of which the last casualties in the regiment were incurred.

The commanding officer returned to 2nd Brigade Headquarters at 1800 hours where he reported to Brigadiers Gibson and Tetley. He learned that the whole operation was concluded successfully and 5th Canadian Armoured Division were preparing to exploit through towards the river Melfa.

Thus ended the battle of the Adolf Hitler Line, a battle in which both Canadian Infantry and our tanks faced very stubborn and fierce resistance. Heavy casualties had been inflicted on the enemy and we sustained, in our turn, serious casualties. It is now known that 1st Canadian Division suffered one thousand casualties in killed, wounded and missing and the N.I.H. lost twenty-five tanks, thirty-four officers and men being killed and thirty-six wounded.

The greatest gallantry and devotion to duty was displayed by all ranks throughout the battle and their determination to support the infantry at all costs has caused the highest praise from all sources.

The regiment is known to have destroyed two Panther Mark V tanks, two Mark IV Specials, one self-propelled 75 mm. gun, one Panther turret emplacement, one 88 mm. anti-tank gun, one 75 mm. anti-tank gun, one 20 mm. dual purpose gun, two armoured machine-gun posts and several snipers. Casualties on enemy infantry could not be computed.

Some six months had been spent by the enemy in constructing this line, emplacements for anti-tank guns and machine-guns being made of steel and concrete and very cleverly sited. Minefields and wire were laid tactically so as to draw on tanks and infantry into definite killing grounds. Tank obstacles were found on the flanks, again to force our tanks into desired areas All artillery and mortar fire had been registered previously, lanes of fire had been cut cleverly in woods and scrub and in some cases large clearings had been made. Camouflaged snipers formed the outposts of the line and must have acted as artillery and mortar observation posts. The static defences of the line were augmented by approximately thirty tanks and self-propelled guns.

At first light on 24th May, 1944, the regiment was put at one hour's notice and ordered to re-organise as quickly as possible on the basis of two Churchill troops and two Sherman troops per fighting squadron. Re-organisation proceeded well during the morning and at 1200 hours the regiment was put at four hours' notice to move.

Reconnaissance during this morning showed that the enemy had withdrawn his remnants from the entire Hitler Line during the early hours of the morning, leaving all heavy equipment in our hands. At first light the 5th Canadian Armoured Division passed through the line and by the evening had pushed elements over the river Melfa. At 1300 hours A B and C squadrons, now re-organised, were concentrated in harbour in the area of the forward assembly area and the collection of the dead had commenced. In the afternoon Brigadier Gibson honoured the regiment by requesting the burial of N.I.H. dead in the 2nd Canadian Brigade Cemetery and congratulatory messages for our part in the action were received from the Canadian Corps Commander, G.O.C. 1st Canadian Division and Brigadier Tetley.

On Thursday evening, 25th May, a burial service was held in the 2nd Canadian Infantry Brigade Cemetery where a plot had been reserved for the North Irish Horse. The cemetery lies about four and a half miles to the south of Pontecorvo and is enclosed on three sides by oak trees, the open side looking across the Liri Valley towards the historic Monastery Hill and Mount Cairo.

It was fitting that the men of the North Irish Horse should be
· buried near their Canadian comrades in arms, who fought and fell with them in the Adolf Hitler Line. The 23rd of May took heavy toll of the regiment. Thirty-two of our friends were buried in that plot of land.

A simple and moving Service of Consecration was held at the cemetery and the site has left associations deeply imprinted upon the minds of the Canadian and British Troops concerned.

29th May—The regiment concentrated at Pofi after a long and slow approach march.

30th May—After another difficult night march squadrons moved up Route 6 to join up with their infantry.

31st May—During the night, the Edmontons with C squadron, established themselves in Frosinone and by first light B squadron were linked up with the Seaforths just north of Frosinone and A squadron with the Princess Pat's just south of that town.

The 2nd Canadian Brigade was ordered soon afterwards to capture and hold Monte Radicino as soon as possible so as to secure the right flank of 1st Canadian Brigade which was advancing up the western side of the valley. The Brigadier ordered the Edmontons to carry out this task as soon as possible and an Order Group was held immediately. It was decided to attack with the Edmontons, supported by C squadron under Major P. Welch, M.C., with A squadron to support C squadron and protect their right flank. A section of the R.E. Troop of 25th Tank Brigade was asked for and arrived at 1130 hours.

At this time all movement in the valley was being subjected to enemy artillery and mortar fire. One battery of the Royal Devon Yeomanry was put in support of C squadron and the advance on the objective started at 1145 hours. The commanding officer ordered B squadron commander to push two troops forward to a small vine-covered feature from which they could control the left flank of the attack. At 1300 hours, after slow progress owing to very difficult country, C squadron were held up by a large demolition on Highway 6. Major Welch gave the Section of R.Es. the task of making a crossing of the stream to the East of the demolition, and, with the help of the Infantry Pioneers, this was completed and C squadron across in 75 minutes from starting. Very little opposition was encountered on the right of the objective, fire coming from a convent situated on a small but steep knoll· One company of infantry and two troops of C squadron were despatched to take this feature and, during this operation, the tanks of C squadron and Shermans of A squadron fired a lot of ammunition at the feature. One Sherman of C squadron turned upside down in a deep hole but no casualties were incurred throughout the day.

1st June—The village of Ferentino was cleared of the enemy and the day was spent in carrying out essential maintenance. The regiment was involved in no further operations until Lieut -Col. E V. Strickland, M.M., acting commanding officer, handed over command of the regiment to Lieut.-Col. The Lord O'Neill, who re-joined the regiment from hospital on the 3rd June, 1944.

4th June—Lieut.-Col. Strickland left the regiment to return to command the 145th Regiment R.A.C.

6th June—Orders were received that 25th Army Tank Brigade would come under command of 4th British Division and the N.I.H. were to be affiliated to 28th Infantry Brigade commanded by Brigadier A. Montague Douglas Scott, D.S.O., an old friend of the Regiment from the time when he had commanded the 1st Battalion of the Irish Guards.

During the afternoon Major-General Dudley Ward, D.S.O., outlined his plan for the advance of 4th British Division from the area of Valmontone, north through Tivoli, which had been taken that morning by the French from a south-westerly direction. The 28th Infantry Brigade and N.I.H. were to be in reserve.

7th June—The regiment received orders during the evening to move to a harbour area near Valmontone. Affiliations were arranged with battalions of 28th Infantry Brigade but this brigade was not used and on 10th June the 8th Indian Infantry Division took over the advance from 4th Division and N.I.H. came under command of the 17th Indian Infantry Brigade.

Owing to its being impossible to provide transporters the regiment remained in the area of Valmontone until 16th June. This period was used for rest and maintenance and " Liberty " runs into Rome were organized. On arrival in Rome one truck driver, asked of another where he could park the truck, was informed that he could put it " by the bombed-out building " ; the reference point was the Coliseum !

On 15th June orders were received from 25th Army Tank Brigade that a composite force comprising all Shermans was to come under command of the 8th Indian Division. A composite squadron was formed under Major P. Welch, M.C., and together with the reconnaissance troop, carried out a three-day approach march involving a journey of one hundred and thirty-eight miles. On the 18th June this force reached Bastia and found the enemy were about five miles away and withdrawing under pressure.

19th June—Two troops under Lieut. J. Rogers and Lieut. D. Hunt respectively, advanced in support of the 6th Indian Lancers towards the village of Ripa. It was thought that the enemy would have evacuated this place during the night but on reaching the western approaches it was found to be held. Lieut. Roger's troop lost two tanks but Lieut. Hunt's troop in supporting an infantry attack on Ripa had a good shoot and inflicted casualties on the enemy. Later on this day Lieut. Hubbard's troop supported a company of infantry on to Palazzo, a ridge with a large house on it.

20th June—Two troops under Lieut. H. E. Irwin, M.C., and Lieut. P. A. Garstin respectively, supported two companies of the 1st-12th Frontier Force Regiment on to two ridges. Zero for this attack was at 1830 hours. The attack was preceded by a barrage and smoke programme. The smoke programme proved to be too heavy and both troops found difficulty in contacting their infantry. However, with the help of an Infantry Liaison Officer this was achieved and by last light the troops had put their companies on to the objectives. The commanding officer of the 1st-12th Frontier Force Regiment arranged with Major Welch to go forward to the second objective at 0500 hours the next day to reconnoitre for an attack across the Grande River on to a feature called Colombella.

21st June—At first light both Lieut. Irwin and Lieut. Garstin rang up to say that their companies wished to carry out mopping up operations to the north of their positions. Plans for this were made and soon put into force. Major Welch rang up Lieut. Irwin to find out how he was getting on and was told, " The place is full of Germans running around in circles ; I never saw so many." He was told to deal with them, which he did effectively, killing between thirty and forty and taking six prisoners. Lieut. Garstin also had a good shoot and knocked out two machine-gun posts.

At 1100 hours the Brigade Commander of the 17th Indian Brigade under whom the regiment was working, now decided to change the axis of advance to a road further east ; the original intention having been to advance up a road which clung to the left bank of the Tiber. He asked for the remainder of the squadron to be prepared to attack with the 1st Battalion Royal Fusiliers. Major Welch started making plans with the commanding officer of the Royal Fusiliers. At 1500 hours the brigade commander informed the commanding officer, N.I.H., that ammunition for the guns was in short supply. In view of this the commanding officer suggested that the attack be put off to the next day when it would be possible to withdraw the two troops who were under command of the 1st-12th Frontier Force Regiment and support the Royal Fusiliers' attack with the whole composite squadron. The brigade commander readily agreed.

The commanding officer took the opportunity of this lull to relieve Major Welch who had been on the go for some time and Major W. M. Mackean, M.C., was placed in command of the composite squadron. The plan of attack was now re-made on the basis of having the whole squadron. At last light Lieut. Irwin's and Lieut. Garstin's troops withdrew, having been in their tanks for twenty-six hours and having done excellent work.

22nd June—A co-ordinating conference was to be held with the brigade commander at 1100 hours but at this conference it was notified that the divisional commander had decided to postpone the attack. We were most disappointed to hear this as we all felt very confident of success. News had been received that the 3rd Hussars were to relieve N.I.H. and the divisional commander felt that with a whole regiment of armour he could carry out a deeper penetration than with a composite squadron.

The brigade commander asked the commanding officer if he could arrange to carry out an offensive harassing shoot with the squadron. We were only too delighted to have a really good go with the 75 mm. Major Mackean was instructed to contact all four battalion commanders on our front and to shoot up any place that was bothering them. A thousand rounds of ammunition were fired and as a result four parties of the enemy carrying Red Cross flags appeared at various points on the front.

23rd-24th June—On the 23rd a further shoot was carried out and on the 24th the hand-over was made to the 3rd Hussars. During the whole time on Ripa the squadron looked across the Tiber to Perugia which fell to 6th Armoured Division on the 20th of the month.

The Sherman tanks were left behind at Bastia while the remainder of the regiment came north to Narni. Those who had been with the composite Sherman squadron returned by road and the regiment was concentrated two miles outside the town of Narni. The regiment was informed that there would probably be an interval of three weeks and this was used to carry out training and a good deal of shooting, while as many people as possible went on 48 hours leave to Rome.

The regiment was informed that the Sherman tanks left at Bastia would be replaced by a " mock up " 75 mm. Churchill and these started arriving on the 10th of July. The Regiment was the first Churchill regiment to be given this type of tank and although it had not the gunnery gadgets of the Sherman it was welcomed by all ranks.

On 16th July news came through that it was likely the regiment would operate with 4th British Infantry Division in the near future. It was hoped that we should be with 28th Infantry Brigade, commanded by Brigadier Montague Scott, D.S.O. Happily this wish was fulfilled. The following battle report was submitted covering the operations during the period 17th July till 9th August, 1944.

BATTLE REPORT

On 17th July orders were received from 25th Army Tank Brigade that the Regiment would move to a concentration area near Arezzo On the 18th all tanks left on transporters and information was received that 25th Brigade would come under command of 4th British Infantry Division and that N.I.H. would be affiliated with 28th Infantry Brigade. The wheeled transport moved to Arezzo on 19th July.

20th July—The Commanding Officer and Squadron Leaders reported to Headquarters, 28th Brigade, and affiliations were arranged as follows :—

A squadron with the 2nd King's Liverpools (2nd Kings).

B squadron with the 2nd Somerset Light Infantry (Som. L.I.)

C squadron with the 2nd-4th Hampshire Regiment (2-4 Hamps).

During the night 20th-21st July, C squadron moved to the area of Bucine.

21st July—Regimental Headquarters moved to headquarters 28th Brigade.

Major R. D. Morton reported to Lieut.-Col. Mitchell, commanding 2nd-4th Hamps, who asked him to concentrate his squadron in the area of Montevarchi by 1600 hours. The commanding officer of 2nd-4th Hamps outlined his plan for the following day. A patrol was to go to Meleto during the night of 21st-22nd July and if this place was found to be unoccupied, No. 2 Troop under Lieut. Hubbard, was to support A company in the advance through Meleto and up the divisional axis. If the patrol found Meleto occupied then Nos. 1 and 2 Troops would support A company from the start line on to the ridge—known as Points 211 and 217—as a first objective and into Meleto as a second objective.

22nd July—The patrol found Meleto held and Nos. 1 and 2 Troops moved forward to the start line to cross it at 0600 hours. The bridge was blown and a diversion had to be found. Further delays were occasioned by Lieut. Hubbard's tank overturning at the crossing. It was decided to push the infantry ahead without the tanks. The wadi crossing on the start line was a difficult one and Sjt. McQueen, of the Reconnaissance Troop, was killed while guiding the tanks across on foot. By 1200 hours all tanks were across. Lieut.-Colonel Mitchell now decided to pass B company through A company on to the western end of Meleto ridge, the tanks to support from the ridge at Points 211 and 217. No. 2 Troop, consisting of two Churchills and commanded by Lieut. H. E. Irwin, M.C., in a Sherman, together with No. 4 Troop and Capt. C. M. Thomas, M.C., in a close support tank, took up positions on the ridge, Points 211 and 217 and supported the infantry onto the area C. Fiazzoie. As soon as the infantry were on the objective, No. 3 Troop, under Lieut. J. Foster, was to cross the wadi and move up to them. The infantry reached the objective but Lieut. Foster found difficulty in finding a crossing of the river. In the course of the reconnaissance for the crossing,

Cpl. Cunningham's tank was hit three times by a 75 mm. firing from Meleto but was not penetrated. Eventually a crossing was found and both Nos. 2 and 3 Troops joined the infantry. Any movement eastwards towards Meleto encountered heavy machine-gun and self-propelled gun fire and it was, therefore, decided to consolidate the position gained. Nos. 2 and 3 Troops remained with the infantry during the night. Plans were made for the 2nd Kings, supported by A squadron, to attack Meleto at first light on the 22nd. The commanding officer of 2nd Kings decided to attack from the south-east but as there was no crossing for the tanks from this direction a two-axis attack was agreed to.

23rd July—Major R. J. Griffith, M.C., and A squadron found great difficulty in getting over the three river crossings which had been damaged by C squadron crossing on the previous day and the commanding officer had to ask for H Hour to be put back. At 0530 hours information was received from Italian sources that the Germans had evacuated Meleto.

Two companies of the 2nd Kings and A squadron N.I.H. moved on the village. As soon as they were in the village infantry and tanks were both subjected to heavy shelling, mortar and machine-gun fire as well as self-propelled gun fire from close range and from three sides. Any forward move was clearly impossible. Sjt. Barbour shot up and knocked out one self-propelled gun and Lieut. J. Waters, in a Sherman, was about to engage another when his tank was hit by an H.E. shell and his operator was wounded. By the time his vision had cleared the gun had gone. Counter-attack positions were taken up by the infantry and tanks.

24th July—Infantry patrols during the night found the enemy to be still in the surrounding country with strong positions on Points 234 and 236. All A squadron tanks engaged this area during the morning. In the afternoon the area was engaged by all C squadron 75 mm. Churchills plus three Shermans of the Reconnaissance Troop. Great damage to houses was caused and infantry patrols that night found the area vacated.

As the country north-east of Meleto was of a jungle nature and offered excellent defensive positions to the enemy, Brigadier Scott decided to shift the axis of his advance. The Somersets were to advance supported by B squadron.

The first objective was to be the line of a track running east to west and the second objective the line of the river. A route reconnaissance was made in the afternoon and the track was found to be possible. At last light Nos. 1 and 2 Troops with two tanks of squadron H.Q. Fighting Troop moved into harbour.

25th July—At 0530 hours No. 1 troop moved out of harbour with a company of the Som. L.I. The going proved hard and the tanks were guided by personnel on foot behind the leading platoons. The first objective was reached without opposition. No. 2 Troop and one tank from Squadron H.Q. then moved out of harbour on the same axis.

A further advance was made and no opposition was met until the leading infantry were at Point 315 where they were engaged

41

by machine-gun fire. No. 1 troop engaged suspected localities with machine-gun and H.E. fire and was then ordered into a counter-attack role on the road junction nearby. By last light the leading companies were on the line of the track and Point 330 as well as Point 315. No. 2 troop moved into a covering position on the Camporeggi Ridge. A protective platoon was provided for the night's harbour.

26th July—No. 1 troop was not engaged during the day but No. 2 Troop engaged enemy occupied houses in the Poggio Secco area, which had been observed from Meleto. Good results were obtained, air bursts being particularly effective. Enemy were seen to evacuate casualties. This position had been bothering 2nd Kings but direct fire from the tanks from a flank finally dislodged them.

During the day Partisan information indicated a possible crossing of the deep ravine ahead, the ordinary bridge having been blown. A patrol, one platoon in strength, went out at last light accompanied by Capt. R. S. H. Sidebottom, and Sjt. Ridley of the Royal Engineers Section attached to B squadron. They reported that the crossing was difficult but possible after demolitions.

27th July—At 0530 hours the infantry moved forward and crossed the river. The Royal Engineers went down immediately afterwards and made the demolitions. No. 2 troop moved into a position to give covering fire along the track. No. 1 troop went down to the crossing but both leading tanks broke tracks on the approach to the crossing and the troops did not cross until 1500 hours. Immediately after they crossed No. 2 troop went over without incident and prepared to support another advance. These two troops leaguered in the area and in spite of heavy nebelwerfer fire suffered no casualties. It was decided that 2nd-4th Hamps with C squadron should] capture Martino the following day.

28th July—The plan was that 2nd-4th Hamps were to take Martino and the surrounding heights, supported by the tanks, first from Pavelli and then, if possible, from one of the heights —Point 531. A bad wadi was encountered but after an hour's hard work by the R.Es. four tanks were got safely across and the remainder positioned on the hill overlooking Martino. The infantry reached Palagio, but it was obvious that all movement forward of this place was observed by enemy forces holding the high ground at San Lucia. Lieut.-Col. Mitchell thus decided to attack Point 505 which, after heavy fighting, was occupied and eventually consolidated. During this attack C squadron engaged targets in Martino and Nos. 3 and 4 Troops advanced to San Andrea in an endeavour to reach Point 531. However, the ground was impossible and it was decided to leave them there for the night.

29th July—The 2nd-4th Hamps were ordered to probe forward with a view to occupying Point 531, but were subjected to heavy fire and the attack was postponed until the following morning.

During the morning Nos. 3 and 4 troops shot up targets in the Martino area and the forward observation officer directed his guns on to the same area in the afternoon. In the process a lot of counter shelling was experienced and consequently the tanks withdrew to a more sheltered position for the night.

30th July—At 0430 hours the 2nd-4th Hamps launched their attack on Point 531 and by 0600 hours the enemy had been driven from the feature. The 2nd Kings passed through 2nd-4th Hamps. A squadron were not able to accompany them as no movement for tanks past the San Andrea area was possible and Martino was still in enemy hands.

31st July—The Somersets supported by B squadron captured Martino, and A squadron, plus two Shermans, passed through on to Point 531. It proved impossible for A squadron to follow 2nd Kings across the hills so all the 75 mm. Churchills, plus the two Shermans, engaged targets across the river on the 6th British Armoured Divisional front. Targets included a headquarters, two gun positions, a nebelwerfer position and transport on Route 69.

As this position gave such excellent observation in front of the 6th Armoured Division, Lieut J Waters, and the two Sherman tanks were left at Point 531 on the three following days. Liaison was affected with 6th Armoured Division forward observation officer and flash spotter, and Lieut. Waters fired off an average of 200 rounds per gun per day for the next three days.

1st August—Sjt. Ridley and his R.E. section repaired three demolitions in readiness for the next day's advance. C squadron was moved up to Raggio a La Croche. The brigade axis now passed through a long defile which it was thought likely the enemy would defend.

2nd August—Plans were made for an attack by C squadron with one troop of A squadron to give right flank protection and also to shoot up part of the area by moonlight. Enemy fire from this flank had been giving the 2nd Kings trouble. Later on this day information was received that the enemy were likely to withdraw.

3rd August—The Somersets continued the advance with B squadron to San Polo. Major Griffith's jeep ran over a Schu mine whilst on a reconnaissance to San Polo, the only damage being a buckled wheel. In the afternoon the 2nd-4th Hamps and C squadron passed through the Somersets and reached San Donatino, and still no contact had been made. In order to try and regain contact Lieut. Irwin with a section of the Reconnaissance Troop, and a section of the 2nd-4th Hamps Carrier Platoon under command, was ordered to make a reconnaissance of the area Bagno a Ripoli-Balatio—Belmonte. At Belmonte this force encountered the enemy and the point Honey tank was knocked out by a Bazooka. Lieut. Irwin reported enemy strength as about fifteen and that they were mostly in houses. A medium concentration was asked for but the brigade commander of the 12th Infantry Brigade refused to allow this fire as he was uncertain of the location of his forward infantry to the west of Belmonte. In consequence, Lieut. Irwin was ordered to shoot up the area with 75 mm. and then withdraw as he had completed his task.

4th August—The 2nd-4th Hamps and C squadron moved forward about 0500 hours and their advance continued throughout the morning, with tactical headquarters moving in jeeps behind the forward companies. It was strangely quiet and no shot was fired by either the enemy or ourselves. Large scale demolitions were encountered and three prisoners of war picked up, obviously intending to desert. Identification was the 104th Panzer Grenadier Regiment. By 1215 hours the two forward companies had reached La Croche, overlooking Florence. At this juncture the infantry brigadier arrived and ordered that the advance should not continue beyond Vicchio. Meantime the squadron were on the move to a concentration area at Le Carti. Heavy shelling was encountered along the route and caused eight casualties in the Reconnaissance Troop and one in No. 3 troop of C squadron. Infantry patrols reported the high ground to the west as being firmly held by the enemy who were heard digging in during the night.

5th August—It was now clear that the enemy were going to make a stand on the high ground between Pontassieve, M. Pilli and Monte Acuto. The Somersets got a foothold by taking M. Pilli and the day was spent in making plans for a moonlight attack by the Somersets on to the Incontro feature. Two troops of B squadron moved into fire positions to give moonlight fire support. On the left infantry patrols were sent to Badia and Point 431 but encountered Spandau fire and mortaring. It was thus appreciated that the enemy were holding the high ground to the east in some strength (approximately company areas), and that any attack on Point 431 must be launched from the ridges of Points 516 and 424. C squadron's activity for the day was confined to a shoot by Nos. 2 and 4 Troops, with one close support tank, against targets during the afternoon. Between 2345 and 2359 hours Nos. 1 and 3 troops shot Besa on fixed lines as a diversion for the attack by the Somersets.

6th August—The attack by the Somersets on Incontro met heavy opposition and the forward companies were unable to reach their objective and had to withdraw. Later on this day orders were received that the 10th Infantry Brigade would take over from the 28th Brigade and be responsible for clearing the country south of the river Arno. The commanding officer was instructed to give all support he could to the 10th Brigade as, owing to road restrictions, it was impossible for the affiliated regiment, the 51st R. Tanks, to accompany the infantry.

On the left, infantry patrols were sent out and No. 2 troop of C squadron was moved into a fire position with complete command of Point 431. In the early afternoon a Spandau opened up on an ambulance jeep at La Croche and was immediately observed from our observation post and engaged successfully by

No. 2 troop. Three enemy were observed to walk down the hill and pick up a wounded man from the area engaged. This direct shooting was obviously most effective. At 1400 hours the Sherman troop went into action at Antella and shelled the Incontro area.

7th August—The commanding officer reported to Brigadier S. N. Shoesmith, D.S.O., O.B.E., who informed him that the 2nd Battalion Duke of Cornwall's Light Infantry (2nd D.C.L.I.) would attack Incontro and that he would like the tanks to support in the first place from the area of Point 516. The commanding officer, accompanied by Major W. M. Mackean, M.C., made a detailed ground reconnaissance. It was clear that tanks could give excellent support from the area of Point 516 but in order to do so would have to be in positions entirely exposed to an unknown right flank. It was decided that Major Mackean would place Lieut. Irwin's Sherman troop under his command and that this troop was to be given the sole task of right flank observation and protection. In addition, a 75 mm. troop of A squadron was to take up a fire position to give further right flank protection whilst a further 75 mm. troop of C squadron should take up positions and be ready to engage targets on Point 436. The commanding officer returned to headquarters, 10th Infantry Brigade, and informed Brigadier Shoesmith that the tanks could give excellent support and that he thought tanks could make the ascent to Incontro although he could not guarantee this. Major Mackean then reported to Lieut.-Col. Musson, D.S.O., who was commanding the 2nd D.C.L.I. and the plan was worked out in detail. The plan was a two-axis attack, the infantry attacking along the line of a re-entrant and the tanks along the axis of Point 516, Point 424 and Incontro. The attack was timed for 0525 hours on the 8th of August. Capt. R. S. H. Sidebottom went with the scout car to headquarters, D.C.L.I. in a farm and acted as liaison officer. A very extensive artillery fire plan was laid on. The commanding officer approached Lieut.-Colonel Brocklehurst, who was commanding the 30th Field Regiment R.A. and asked him if he could spare a forward observation officer for the following day's attack. Lieut.-Colonel Brocklehurst most kindly agreed and this F.O.O. was with B squadron by 1100 hours.

THE ATTACK ON INCONTRO—

8th August—B squadron laagured for the night, 7th-8th August, except for No. 1 Troop which was separated from the remainder of the squadron by an impassible cliff. At 0500 hours on the 8th, Nos. 4 and 5 troops, two tanks of H.Q. Fighting Troop, a F.O.O. tank and the Reconnaissance Troop Shermans moved out of harbour in that order. The troops were in position by 0545 hours ; No. 4 troop on a ridge 150 yards north of Point 516 ; No. 5 Troop, the F.O.O. tank and close support tank on Point 516 ; the Shermans on Point 508 and No. 1 Troop on their left.

Heavy firing was heard from the direction of the objective as soon as the troops were in position and when it was confirmed that our infantry were only as far as the western wall of the monastery, No. 5 Troop quickly engaged likely enemy positions with 75 mm. H.E. and the close support tank with the 3-in. Howitzer. The F.O.O. and other tank commanders spotted what they thought was a flash of a self-propelled gun from the north east and high velocity shells landed in the area. All tanks then moved on to the western slopes of the ridge, but spasmodic shelling by medium guns was experienced throughout the day.

The infantry re-formed and put in a second attack along the southern wall. When they had covered about half the distance the forward tank troops observed the enemy forming up for a counter-attack along the south eastern wall. As soon as it was confirmed that these were not our own troops, devastating fire was opened by No. 5 Troop with 75 mm. H.E. and by Nos. 1 and 4 Troops with machine-gun and 6-pounder H.E. The counter-attack dispersed. The enemy counter-attack force numbered about thirty. The fire brought down by the tanks was at one place only fifty yards ahead of our own infantry. This was possible due to the excellent infantry communications and the tank liaison officer at the infantry battalion headquarters, being able to transmit these positions to all tanks on the tank wireless net. Twelve enemy dead were found subsequently in the area where the tank fire had been directed.

An enemy machine-gun nest was reported in the monastery tower and this was rapidly demolished by armoured piercing fire from all the forward tank troops. A fresh infantry plan was then made for the third company to attack at 1050 hours and for five minutes before this attack was launched further concentrations of H.E. and machine-gun fire from the tanks were put down along the south eastern wall. The commanding officer of the D.C.L.I. then asked that once the company attack was launched, a troop should try and get forward to Incontro. Major Mackean ordered Lieut. Foott to make a reconnaissance on foot for a route down the hill. Lieut. Foott reported that he had found a way but that the going was bad and that his troop would be very exposed to the right. Major Mackean then went down personally on foot. These route reconnaissances were by no means easy as all had to be done on a forward slope which was under continuous shell fire and in full view of the enemy. Major Mackean discovered a way which gave defilade from the right. Lieut. Foott was then ordered to make the descent and then the ascent to Incontro. Lieut. Foott manœuvred his troop down an appalling slope and then, covered by No. 5 troop on the forward ridge of Point 516 and No. 2 troop from the ridge behind, he worked his way up the slopes of the objective to the walls of the monastery. About this time the F.O.O., Captain Sedgwick, was wounded in the face by a mortar shell while out of his tank.

No. 2 troop then passed through No. 5 Troop and, following No. 4 troop tracks, joined them on the objective. Almost as soon as they had arrived, Lieut. Behr and Tpr. Fuller were wounded by shell fire whilst out of their tanks. It was decided to evacuate Tpr. Fuller back in the tank the way they had come but in spite of the guiding by Sjt. Verso of No. 5 troop, they went off their course and ran into a party of Germans armed with a Bazooka. Sjt. Verso, who was on the outside of the tank at the time and Cpl. Reynolds who was commanding it, were wounded by the projectile which passed between their heads. Sjt. Verso jumped off the tank and took cover. Cpl. Reynolds fell into the turret and L.-Cpl. Gault, the driver, closed down, and with the aid of Troopers Johnson and Fuller, fired the 75 mm., traversed the turret and got the front Besa into action. He then got the tank going and took it up the hill and rejoined his troop. Shortly after this Tpr. Martin, J., was wounded by shell fragments while outside his tank.

As a result of this attack three enemy officers and sixty-nine other ranks were taken prisoner and twenty dead counted in the monastery area. The capture of this feature forced the enemy to leave all their positions south of the river Arno.

At 1800 hours Major Mackean and Capt. Sidebottom were ordered to return to regimental headquarters and then, with the commanding officer, went to the headquarters of the 2nd Surreys to plan for an attack on Point 437.

9th August—The 2nd Surreys put in their attack with B squadron ready to support, but the enemy had gone with few exceptions, and the tanks had only one target of twelve fleeing Germans.

GOTHIC LINE.

REGIMENTAL HEADQUARTERS

Lieutenant-Colonel The Lord O'Neill		..	Commanding Officer
Major P. Welch, M.C. ..	..	..	Second-in-Command
Captain M. B. Pope, M.C.	..	..	Adjutant
Captain J. B. Behr ..	..	..	Liaison Officer
Lieut. R. B. M. King ..	..	..	Signals Officer
Lieut. J. Maxwell ..	..	..	Intelligence Officer

Sjt. Hamilton   Tpr. O'Regan
Sjt. Irvine   Tpr. Smith
Cpl. Cox   Tpr. Prince
Cpl. Keenan   Tpr. Sherer
Cpl. Reaks   Tpr. Turnham
Cpl. Murray   Tpr. Horrocks
L/Cpl. Plenderleith   Tpr. Gothorp
L/Cpl. McComish   Tpr. Wray
Tpr. Allen   Tpr. Noble
Tpr. Ging   Tpr. Hamilton, W.
Tpr. Kennedy   Tpr. Templeton
Tpr. Lyttle   Tpr. Godden
Tpr. Beveridge   Tpr. McWilliams, J.

MEDICAL GROUP
Captain B. Lush, R.A.M.C.
Cpl. Sleghorne
Tpr. Higgins
Tpr. Holden
Tpr. Strong
Tpr. Chapman

ORDER OF BATTLE

" A " SQUADRON

H.Q. TROOP	No. 1 TROOP	No. 2 TROOP
Major Griffith, M.C.	Sjt. Donaghy	Lieut. Wilson
Sjt. Mitchell	Tpr. Sartin	L/Cpl. Church, M.M.
L/Cpl. Graham, A.	Tpr. Reay	Tpr. Hanshaw
Tpr. Patrick	Tpr. Cree	L/Cpl. Millar
Tpr. Peden	Tpr. Badger	Tpr. McKeague
Capt. Finch Noyes	Cpl. McKee	Sjt. McIlherene
Cpl. Fallis	Tpr. Tarbard	L/Cpl. Moore
Tpr. Connor	Tpr. Martin, M.M.	Tpr. Harrison
L/Cpl. Johnston, M.M.	L/Cpl. Crisp	Tpr. Ranger
Tpr. Stevens	Tpr. Cameron	Tpr. Hines
Sjt. Young	Cpl. Watson	Cpl. Asprey
Tpr. Howard	Tpr. Tyndall	Tpr. Jacobs
Tpr. Green	Tpr. Barr	Tpr. Wesley
L/Cpl. Brown	L/Cpl. Ainsworth	Tpr. Whyte
Tpr. Lynas	Tpr. Tobias	L/Cpl. Sherritt

No. 3 Troop	No. 4 Troop
Lieut. Hunt	Lieut. Norris
Tpr. Morris-Francis	Tpr. Cassells
Tpr. Clarke	Tpr. Rees
L/Cpl. Graham, D.	Tpr. Lang
Tpr. Williams	Tpr. Stokes, B.
Sjt. Graham	Sjt. Ballard
Tpr. Smith	Tpr. Grey
Tpr. Walker	L/Cpl. Robinson
Tpr. Parker	Tpr. Gledhill
Tpr. Calland	Tpr. Lymer

RELIEFS

Lieut. Waters (Comd.)
Cpl. Hutchman (Comd.)
Tpr. Cowan (Operator)
Tpr. Hodson (Gunner)
Tpr. Young (Driver)
Tpr. McWilliams (Driver.)
Tpr. Harding

FITTERS' ECHELON

A.R.V. Crew	Half-Track	
L/Sjt. Jackson	Sjt. Trotter	Tpr. Sherlock
Tpr. Bailey	Cpl. Fuffin	Tpr. Meichen
Tpr. Gallaher	Tpr. Eyre	L/Cpl. Lochart
Tpr. Hawkridge	Tpr. Howat	
Cfn. Mattick, R.E.M.E.		

" A " SQUADRON ECHELON

Capt. R. H. Bowring

S.S.M. Leslie	Tpr. Eakins
S.Q.M.S. Allen	Tpr. Henderson
Sjt. Baird	Tpr. Kane
Sjt. Moore, T.	Tpr. Lissaman
Cpl. Baker	Tpr. Malcolmson
Cpl. Haren	Tpr. Mann
Cpl. Lyne	Tpr. Morrison
Cpl. Lavery	Tpr. Mitchell
L/Cpl. Cunningham	Tpr. McLaughlin
L/Cpl. Cox, R.	Tpr. McCombe
L/Cpl. McKillen	Tpr. Richmond
L/Cpl. Marshall	Tpr. Reynolds
L/Cpl. Patton	Tpr. Sterritt
Tpr. Armstrong	Tpr. Walls
Tpr. Coyle	Tpr. Wardle
Tpr. Cunningham, J.	Tpr. Wesley, H.
Tpr. Duncan, S.	Tpr. Williams
	Tpr. Ward

Fitters	Cooks
Cpl. McIntosh	Cpl. Boyle
Tpr. Barlow	L.U.L.C. Griffiths
Tpr. Barnacle	Pte. Chartres
	Pte. Flynn
	Pte. Hales

49

" B " SQUADRON

H.Q. Troop	No. 1 Troop	No. 2 Troop
Major Mackean, M.C.	Lieut. B. E. S. King	Lieut. Fleming
Cpl. Chester	Cpl. Malseed	Cpl. Walls
Tpr. Young	L/Cpl. Cox	L/Cpl. Martin, T.
L/Cpl. Colard	Tpr. Burton	Tpr. Shanks
Tpr. Dawson, N.H.	Tpr. Chilton	L/Cpl. Gault
Capt. Sidebottom	Cpl. McCullough	Sjt. McAughtry
Tpr. Loxdale	L/Cpl. Beatty	Tpr. Walker, E.
Tpr. Knight	Tpr. Perkins	Tpr. Kerr
Cpl. Hayward	Tpr. Gilligan	Tpr. Doupe
Tpr. Clatworthy	Tpr. Bateston	Tpr. Harrow
Sjt. Burns	Sjt. Maxwell	Sjt. Buchanan
Tpr. Sharples	Tpr. Mitchell	Cpl. Wiggins
Tpr. Wood, J.	L/Cpl. Gifford	Tpr. Rexworthy
Tpr. Dalzell	Tpr. James	Tpr. Cawley
Tpr. Gamble	Tpr. Johnson	Tpr. Moore, H. J.

No. 4 Troop	No. 5 Troop
Lieut. Foott	Sjt. Cheater
L/Cpl. Fennell	Tpr. Macartney
Tpr. Webb	L/Cpl. Darville
L/Cpl. Giboney	L/Cpl. Wallace
Tpr. Fitzgerald	Tpr. Gardiner
Cpl. McCalmont	Lieut. Mahon
Tpr. Dorman	L/Cpl. Marcham
Tpr. Bradfield	Cpl. Keville
L/Cpl. Moore	L/Cpl. Binstead
Tpr. Holt	Tpr. O'Keefe
Sjt. Bullick	Sjt. Verso
Tpr. Glass	Tpr. Hamilton
Tpr. Bowers	Tpr. Newman
Tpr. Robinson	Tpr. Abbott
Tpr. Moore, H. J.	Tpr. White, V. N.

FORWARD ECHELON

Fitters	A.R.V. Crew
Sjt. Holmes	L/Cpl. Hughes
Cpl. Day	L/Cpl. Beatty
Tpr. Brindle	Tpr. Handley
L/Cpl. Wallace	Tpr. Gilligan
L/Cpl. Russell	Tpr. Donaghy

Scout Car	Jeep
Tpr. Griffiths	Tpr. Grant, W.

" B " SQUADRON ECHELON

Capt. W. R. Hern

S.S.M. Humston
S.Q.M.S. Burke
Sjt. Fleming
Cpl. Nelson
Cpl. Crealey
Cpl. Graham
Cpl. Lowry
Cpl. McKenzie
L/Cpl. Gaston
L/Cpl. Duckers
L/Cpl. Miller
L/Cpl. Dunlop
Tpr. Vance
Tpr. McIlveen
Tpr. Hassard
Tpr. Greenfield
Tpr. White, J. A.

Tpr. Fell
Tpr. Wilson
Tpr. Fletcher
Tpr. Mollan
Tpr. Bourne
Tpr. Clarke
Tpr. Robinson
Tpr. Thompson
Tpr. Pilsworth
Tpr. Saunderson
Tpr. Higgins
Tpr. Allen
Tpr. Cantillon
Tpr. White, J.
Tpr. Moffatt
Tpr. Ceirans
Tpr. Waterson

FITTERS

Cpl. Baillie
Tpr. Andrews
Tpr. Coghlan

COOKS

Cpl. Stevenson
Pte. Jameson
Pte. Murray
Pte. Spiers

" C " SQUADRON

H.Q. TROOP	No. 1 TROOP	No. 2 TROOP
Major R. D. Morton, M.C.	Lieut. A. N. MacCleary	Lieut. R. A. Hubbard
L/Cpl. Green, H.U.	Tpr. Williams, P.	Cpl. Owens
Cpl. Sloan	Tpr. McAloon	Tpr. Goulburn
Sjt. Stevenson	Cpl. Gilpin	L/Cpl. James
Tpr. Burton, S.	Tpr. Neilson, M.M.,	Tpr. Coakerill
Capt. C. M. Thomas, M.C.	Sjt. Thacker	Sjt. Bell
Tpr. Tankin	L/Cpl. Gregson	Tpr. Harvey
L/Cpl. Neely	Tpr. Clegg	Tpr. Evans
Cpl. Gale	Tpr. Eastwood	L/Cpl. Neill
Tpr. Gault, W.	L/Cpl. Walker, J.	Tpr. Sibley
Cpl. Ackroyd, J.	Cpl. Coxhill	Cpl. Shaw, H.
L/Cpl. Hinxman	Tpr. McGrath	Tpr. Lodge
Tpr. Ledger	Tpr. Robertson, A.	Tpr. Armstrong
L/Cpl. Cowan	L/Cpl. Winyard	Tpr. Yates
Tpr. Bigg	Tpr. Millson	Tpr. Nolan
	Sjt. Garrigan, M.M.	

No. 3 Troop	No. 4 Troop
Lieut. J. Foster	Lieut. M. L. Bexon
Cpl. Cunningham	L/Cpl. Boyd
Tpr. Bateson	Tpr. Griffin
L/Cpl. Wilson, F.	Cpl. Hamilton
Tpr. Gray	Tpr. Gore, B.
Lieut. D. R. King	
Sjt. Kennedy, M.M.	Sjt. Baker
L/Cpl. Pollard	Tpr. Harper, R.
Tpr. Lambie	Tpr. Wardle
Tpr. Richardson	L/Cpl. Dougall
Tpr. McCrea	Tpr. Tattersall
Cpl. Traynor	L/Sjt. Williams
L/Cpl. Peters	Tpr. Warnock
Tpr. Wattam	Tpr. Leech
Tpr. Wilson, J.	L/Cpl. Jefferson
Tpr. Holmes, F.	Tpr. Parfitt
	Sjt. Christie

RELIEFS

Tpr. Morrison, D.G.
Tpr. O'Neill, P. G.
Tpr. Salmon, E.
Tpr. Hellawell, H.
Tpr. Aldridge, K.
Tpr. Darbyshire, J.
Tpr. Fort, A.
Tpr. Rodgers, W.
Tpr. Dyer, E.
Tpr. Wilson, T.
Tpr. Smithdale, A.
L/Cpl. Carter, A. E.

FITTERS

Sjt. Gettings	L/Sjt. Stewart, J. M.M.
Cpl. McAteer	Cpl. Mogey
L/Cpl. Green	Tpr. Martin
Tpr. Lusty	Tpr. McNeill
Tpr. Hill	Tpr. Davis
Tpr. McBay	Tpr. Maycock
Cfn. Skilleter, R.E.M.E.	Tpr. Harrison (Jeep)

" C " SQUADRON ECHELON

Capt. D. Whelan	Capt. F. A. Norris
S.S.M. Bumstead	Sjt. Murray
Cpl. McLernon	L/Cpl. Dixon
Tpr. Bishop	Tpr. Chartres
Tpr. Hamilton	Tpr. Darragh
Tpr. O'Clery	Tpr. Taylor, K.
Tpr. Spellman	Tpr. Jones
Tpr. McQuilkin	Sjt. Sykes
L/Cpl. Harper, S.	L/Cpl. Grindlay
Tpr. McDowell	Tpr. Devlin
Tpr. Scott	Tpr. Small

S/Sjt. Derrick, H. W.
(R.E.M.E.)
S/Sjt. Medwin, D. H.
(R.E.M.E.)
Tpr. Appleyard, N.

H.Q. SQUADRON

TANK AND SCOUT CAR CREWS

Capt. H. E. Irwin, M.C. Lt. E. D. Bullick

Sjt. Phillips	Sjt. Craig
Sjt. Lytle	Sjt. Wingfield
Cpl. Lester	Sjt. Perioli, S.
L/Cpl. Duke	Cpl. Brown, H.
L/Cpl. Taylor, F.	L/Cpl. Hadley
L/Cpl. Brown, J.	Cpl. Patterson
Tpr. Goulburn	Tpr. Bane
Tpr. Robinson	Tpr. Field
Tpr. Critchley	Tpr. Morrison
Tpr. Mooney	Tpr. McCann
Tpr. Andrewan	Tpr. Smith
Tpr. Anderson, C.	Tpr. Creighton
Tpr. Lang	Tpr. Taylor, L.
Tpr. Jackson	Tpr. Snowdon
Tpr. Hanna, D.	
Tpr. Wilson, J.	
Cpl. Greene	Cpl. Beal
L/Cpl. Simpson	Cpl. Rogers
L/Cpl. Shillito	Tpr. Bibby
Tpr. Creedon	Tpr. Phillips
Tpr. Campbell	Tpr. Anderson, F.
Tpr. Mavitty	
L/Cpl. Casey	Tpr. Catton
L/Cpl. McDougall	Tpr. Fisher
L/Cpl. Greenwood	Tpr. Humphries
Tpr. Steel	Tpr. Askew
Tpr. Hazelton	Tpr. Allen
Tpr. Miller	Tpr. Wilson
Tpr. Taylor	
Tpr. Burrows	Tpr. Day, F.
Tpr. Houlton	
Tpr. Morris	

FITTERS
Cpl. Johnson, A.
Tpr. Fuller
Tpr. Murphy
Tpr. Andrew
Tpr. Porter

H.Q. SQUADRON ECHELON

Major W. G. Lavery   Capt. E. S. Robinson

R.S.M. Fidler
R.Q.M.S. Docksey
S.S.M. Fowler
Sjt. McWilliams
Sjt. Moorhead
Sjt. McGahey
Sjt. McDonagh
Cpl. Cawley
Cpl. Dunlop
Cpl. Pollitt
Cpl. Rocke, S.
Cpl. Stewart, D.
L/Cpl. Cassidy
L/Cpl. Henderson
L/Cpl. Sutherland
L/Cpl. Garner
L/Cpl. Bogle
L/Cpl. Brownlee, J.
L/Cpl. Dermott
L/Cpl. Moore, R.
Tpr. Armstrong, K.
Tpr. Atkinson
Tpr. Andrew
Tpr. Brookes
Tpr. Bott
Tpr. Brenan
Tpr. Copp
Tpr. Dann
Tpr. Donaghy
Tpr. Ferguson

Tpr. Furphy
Tpr. Fiddes
Tpr. Graham
Tpr. Gray
Tpr. Hanna, D.
Tpr. Hawkins
Tpr. Johnson
Tpr. Kennewell
Tpr. Laverty
Tpr. Logue
Tpr. Latimer
Tpr. Lennon
Tpr. Magee
Tpr. McDowell, W.
Tpr. McDonald, D.
Tpr. Morton
Tpr. McDowell, J.
Tpr. Morris
Tpr. Purvis
Tpr. Reynolds
Tpr. Robertson
Tpr. Shipton
Tpr. Smalley
Tpr. Vennard
Tpr. Wylie
Tpr. Sodden
Tpr. Young
Tpr. Knopp
Tpr. Broadhurst
Tpr. Moonan

Q.M.S. (M.) Vanstone, C.
Sjt. Whyte, A.
Cpl. Marsh
Tpr. Thompson, C.
Tpr. Dickenson

Q.M.S. (T.) Scott, E.
Sjt. Smith, R. A. D.
Cpl. Abbott
L/Cpl. Abbott
L/Cpl. Reid
Tpr. Harwood
Tpr. Allard
Tpr. Smith, W.

Sjt. Walford
Tpr. Hodge
Tpr. Fuller, C.

L/Cpl. Toombes, S.
Tpr. Hart
Tpr. Dann

COOKS
Cpl. McKee
Pte. Evans
Pte. Hitchcock
Pte. Crothers

The 4th British Infantry Division were now drawn into army reserve and the regiment was left to concentrate south of Florence. Many of us had looked down upon this city from the southern hills but none of us had an opportunity of a closer inspection for many weeks to come. After three days of rest we were on the road again, this time southward-bound for Perugia. It soon became apparent that very little time would elapse before we must be ready for further operations. Everyone buckled to and work on the tanks went on at high speed during the few days that were allowed us.

The Battle Report for the period 17th August to 4th September read as follows :

15th August—Orders were received that the 25th Army Tank Brigade would come under command of the 46th British Infantry Division with N.I.H. affiliated to the 128th Infantry Brigade. The commanding officer contacted Brigadier D. A. Kendrew, D.S.O., on the 16th August.

17th August—The tanks and wheeled vehicles left Perugia, the former on transporters, and by the 18th the regiment had concentrated in the area of Serra Di Conti.

The period 19th to 25th August was spent in making reconnaissances of tank tracks and awaiting for the area south of the river Metauro to be cleared up.

25th August—The tanks were concentrated in the area of Fratte Rosa.

The 128th Infantry Brigade concentrated on the forward slope going down to the river Metauro. The plan was for the 2nd Hamps. to cross the river at 2300 hours and that A squadron should move from Fratte Rosa at the same hour and cross the river at 0400 hours, 26th August.

26th August—A squadron reached the river without incident but found that the approach to the river would not bear the weight of Churchill tanks and a fresh crossing had to be found. A squadron was across by 0620 hours and joined the 2nd Hamps. at Montefelcino. The problem now for the tanks was to find a crossing of the wadi just ahead. Foot reconnaissance was immediately got under way but it was 1730 hours before a crossing was found. It was too late for the infantry to reach this flank to attack with tanks so it was arranged that the 1st-4th Hamps. should attack Monte San Bartolo.

27th August—The 1st-4th Hamps. captured the feature during the night. B squadron crossed the wadi at dawn and supported 1st-4th Hamps. from the lower slopes of Monte San Bartolo. Several houses in the area were still giving the 1st-4th Hamps. trouble and these were successfully shot up by B squadron.

A squadron now passed through to support the 2nd Hamps. on to a road junction. It was hoped to keep A squadron on the high ground, but, as the going was slow, one troop was detached to move along the road with the infantry. This troop—No. 3— successfully got round two road craters but was eventually held up by a big blow. As progress in the hills was slow the commanding officer ordered the remainder of the squadron down to the road. A bulldozer was rushed up and three more blows filled in before the squadron could reach the road junction. The 2nd Hamps were held up by enemy holding the foothills of Monte Albullo. A quick plan was made. A squadron shot up the whole area and the 2nd Hamps captured the feature by 2100 hours.

28th August—B squadron passed through to support the 1st-4th Hamps to Montegaudio. Further bulldozing was required to get the tanks along the road. The village was found to be occupied by the enemy and street fighting ensued. About thirty prisoners were taken. By 1800 hours the village was clear but the enemy still held Point 414. The infantry found they were unable to advance owing to mortaring, so Nos. 1 and 4 Troops advanced supported by Nos. 2 and 5 Troops. Two machine-gun posts were knocked out on the way but as the infantry were still unable to come up the tanks withdrew at last light.

29th August—The 5th Hampshires advanced to Monte Buseto during the night of 28th-29th August. C squadron were to attempt to cross the watershed to this hill at first light. The going proved very bad but two tanks made the trip. The commanding officer suggested that the remainder of the squadron move round by Ripe, via the road junction to Serra Di Enga. Brigadier Kendrew agreed and the squadron were in the process of moving when orders were received that N.I.H. were to return and come under command of 25th Army Tank Brigade.

30th August—At 0500 hours the Brigadier, 128th Infantry Brigade, asked the commanding officer to accompany him to Colbordolo to make a reconnaissance. It was clear that the Monte Gridolfo feature would have to be taken before tanks or infantry could move across the lower slopes. The commanding officer returned to Monte Grosso where the whole regiment had concentrated the previous evening, with a promise of twenty-four hours' rest and maintenance.

At 1130 hours the commanding officer was ordered to an operation group at Colbordolo. Here he was informed that the 2nd Hamps. were to cross the river Foglia at 1400 hours on this day and Brigadier Kendrew asked for tank support. The commandng officer explained that the tanks were stripped for maintenance but that he would do his utmost to get up tanks. The Reconnaissance troop was ordered to move in one hour's time. Traffic on the road was considerable and the tanks were much delayed. In view of the late hour Brigadier Kendrew decided that he would not use the tanks till the following morning. At 1700 hours orders were received for the regiment to concentrate in the Ripe area and to revert to command of 25th Army Tank Brigade again. A plan was now made for Brigadier Kendrew to command a column of the Divisional Reconnaissance Regiment, the 5th Hamps. and the 142nd Regiment R.A.C. to attempt to burst round the lower slopes of Monte Gridolfo. The commanding officer offered the use of the reconnaissance troop and the armoured " Gin Box."

31st August—At 0500 hours orders were received that N.I.H. were to come under command of the 128th Infantry Brigade again. The commanding officer went forward to Colbordolo and agreed that A squadron should be passed across the river, followed by B squadron. A Sherman-dozer was required to make good a crossing. A squadron crossed and in attempting to make the direct ascent to Monte Le Vecchie encountered a minefield. The commanding officer then ordered that the squadron advance by road. The road up to Monte Le Vecchie proved to be mined and sappers were rushed up to deal with this. A squadron reported a self-propelled gun firing. It was impossible to leave the road and as it was a steep uphill climb no advance was possible. The commanding officer was now ordered to concentrate two squadrons in the area.

1st September—A squadron were ordered to support the advance of the 5th Hamps. to Point 331 and also to help the 1st-4th Hamps. mop up in the area of Monte Gridolfo. These two tasks were successfully fulfilled. At about 1200 hours self-propelled guns were seen approaching Monte Gridolfo from the east and moving south on Meleto. Five self-propelled guns were seen to enter this area. One was engaged at long range by Major R. J. Griffith, M.C. Artillery concentrations were brought down on the area and no movement was seen till late that evening when one self-propelled gun came out on the road and was shot up and knocked out by Lieut. D. Hunt's troop. At about 1400 hours the 5th Hamps. reported an S.P. in Meleto. This gun was engaged by A squadron and driven off. A squadron remained in observation for the remainder of the day in the area of Points 374 and 331.

2nd September—Orders were received that N.I.H. were to come under command of the 138th Infantry Brigade. The regiment concentrated and refuelled in the area of Monte Busco. Brigadier Harding gave out his orders at 2100 hours and the plan was laid on for the 2nd-4th King's Own Yorkshire Light Infantry to form a bridgehead over the river Ventena and the 6th Yorkshire and Lancashires, supported by C squadron, were to advance through them and form a bridgehead over the river Conca, taking the high ground beyond Morciano. One troop was to follow the infantry during moonlight and to be in a position to support them forward on to Morciano, San Andrea and the right. No. 2 troop was detailed for this duty and the remainder of the squadron were to follow at first light. A section of the R.Es. was attached to No. 2 troop, who made their way down the road through the 2nd-4th K.O.Y.L.I. and opened up on enemy in the area of Morciano at 0600 hours the next morning.

3rd September—About 0500 hours the remainder of C squadron moved forward and at 0800 hours No. 3 troop was ordered to cross the Conca, supported by Nos. 2 and 4 troops on the right and left respectively. The tanks reached the crossing which was overlooked by the high ground beyond and were shot at by a self-propelled gun from the area of a cemetery. The infantry nearby were heavily " stonked " and quite unable to advance.

Meantime No. 3 troop—consisting of two tanks plus one from No. 1 troop—had lost two tanks and artillery fire was called for from the forward observation officer to be brought down on the cemetery. No. 4 troop was now moved up to the left of No. 2 troop into a support position but in the process the self-propelled gun knocked out one tank and pinned the other two down.

Fresh plans had now to be made and it was decided to bring a heavy artillery concentration down on the cemetery and to smoke the right flank. Two companies were to advance on to the high ground across the river Conca followed by the remaining tanks, now numbering only five. All went well and the infantry, closely followed by the tanks, reached the objective.

On the right, B squadron advanced across the river Conca at 1200 hours in support of the 2nd Hamps. The advance continued to Point 167 and enemy positions on the ridges to the north-east and north-west were engaged. Some enemy on Point 143 were next shot up and the squadrons remained in forward defence lines in a counter-attack role for the night.

Meanwhile, on the left, A squadron took over from C squadron and supported the 6th York and Lancs into San Clemente and the ridge to the north-west. As the sun got low, self-propelled gunfire was opened on A squadron from Cevelobatte. A squadron suffered no damage.

4th September—On the right B squadron supported the 1st-4th Hamps on to a road junction. Enemy self-propelled guns opened fire from the Coriano ridge. Capt. W. R. Hern's tank was hit, and all members of the crew, bar him, were wounded. On the left A squadron were ordered to support a squadron of the Reconnaissance Regiment in an attack on Coriano. This was later changed to an attack on San Savino. As this attack was about to take place the commanding officer was asked to form a Churchill firm base through which the 1st British Armoured Division would pass. A squadron were ordered to form the base on the ridge from Point 151 to Point 174. As the 10th Hussars passed through an enemy tank was observed on the Coriano ridge and knocked out by No. 3 troop. Three more tanks were engaged. One more was knocked out and the other two got away, though one was hit.

B and A squadrons rallied close behind the San Clemente feature for the night.

The " Intention " paragraph of the 46th British Infantry Division's Operation Order of the 25th August, 1944, read as follows :—

" 46TH DIVISION WILL BREAK THE GOTHIC LINE "

In this period between the 25th August and the 4th September this intention was achieved.

When we reached Colbordolo and looked down on, and across, the river Foglia to Monte Gridolfo, it must be confessed the situation looked anything but pleasant. All houses had been razed to the ground, trees and vines felled and avenues prepared between extensive minefields for a hail of machine-gun fire. Panther turrets were suspected and were later found to be there, though not completely ready for action. The assault across the river Foglia and up the bare slopes beyond appeared suicidal, but the speed of our advance had been such that the enemy had not been able to man this line in sufficient strength and so we passed through. The 128th Infantry Brigade, with which we were co-operating, captured first of all Monte Bardolo, the highest ground on our front between the rivers Metauro and Foglia and then Monte Gridolfo, the most eastern strongpoint of the Gothic Line. At the end of this period Major-General J. L. I. Hawkesworth, C.B., C.B.E., D.S.O., issued the following special order :—

In one week's fighting we have advanced 25 miles and have broken the Gothic Line. We have defeated the greater part of two German divisions, capturing prisoners and inflicting upon the enemy casualties which cannot be less than 3,000.

This is a remarkable achievement and a notable victory.

The Army Commander and the Corps Commander have both asked me to tell you they consider the performance of the Division is marvellous. They have asked me to congratulate and thank you.

For security reasons it is inadvisable for me to tell you here the exact total of casualties incurred. The total is, however, smaller than we have incurred in any comparable battle. The fatigue you have borne so patiently and cheerfully has not been in vain : your sweat has saved much blood.

This victory has been won by your gallantry and selfless and untiring devotion to duty. A well-nigh intolerable strain has, at times, been imposed upon all fighting troops and services. I know of no operation in which such a strain has been imposed upon the services of the Division—and they have met it nobly.

The infantry, so ably supported by the artillery, tanks and Royal Engineers, have shown a gallantry, skill and endurance greater than ever before.

You have all shown that not only have you the tools to finish the job—you have, what is infinitely more important, the skill and the courage to use them. We will finish the job soon.

(Signed) J. L. I. Hawkesworth, Maj.-Gen.

A paragraph of the 128th Infantry Brigade's account of the assault on the Gothic Line reads as follows :—

A special tribute must be paid to squadrons of the N.I.H. Day after day their Churchills forced positions and supported our infantry over appalling tank country. Undaunted, squadron leaders on foot led their tanks up seemingly impossible slopes. One tank actually slipped over and crashed two hundred feet down into a ravine, having turned over six times in its descent.

Once more we had a short spell out of the line, but there was much work to do on the tanks. It was not long before we had news that we should be at it again and we were all delighted to hear that we were to return to our old friends, the 28th Infantry Brigade of the 4th British Infantry Division and the following battle report was submitted, covering the period 12th September to 25th September, 1944 :

After making a firm base on the Coriano and San Savino ridges the 1st British Armoured Division was passed through. Unfortunately Coriano proved a tougher proposition than expected and 1st British Armoured Division were held up. N.I.H. was concentrated just east of San Giovani and much needed maintenance carried out.

12th September—The 25th Army Tank Brigade was put under command of 4th British Infantry Division, under 1st Canadian Corps, with N.I.H. under command of the 28th Infantry Brigade.

The 5th Canadian Armoured Division were to take Coriano. The 51st Battalion R. Tanks were to take Poggio and A and C squadrons N.I.H. were to go through and take Bagli-Patrignano features.

13th September—The attack started and went well but the regiment did not move on this day. On the 14th September the regiment moved to the area of Misano.

15th September—At 0001 hours A squadron followed by C squadron moved forward to cross the river Marano and support the infantry on to the Bagli feature. The plan was for A squadron and the 2nd Kings to move first and make the bridgehead : then take the right of the feature and pass C squadron and the 2nd-4th Hamps through on the left. No. 3 troop A squadron, followed by Nos. 1 and 2 troops, were across by 0630 hours. C squadron quickly followed A squadron across. The 2nd-4th Hamps, working quicker than the 2nd Kings, were on their objective by 0700 hours with C squadron in support. A squadron and the 2nd Kings did not consolidate their objectives till midday. Throughout the day there was very heavy shelling which made all movement difficult. At last light C squadron left Nos. 3 and 4 troops with the 2nd-4th Hamps and B squadron sent Nos. 4 and 5 troops to relieve A squadron, who returned to the Poggio area.

16th September—B squadron moved Nos. 4 and 5 troops to cover Point 137 but the enemy had already made a counter-attack and the tanks remained in a counter-attack position. Very heavy shelling was experienced. Lieut. G. Mahon's tank got a direct hit with a large calibre shell and had to be abandoned but was later recovered. Trooper Mitchell died of wounds. C squadron moved to Patrignano at 2200 hours in preparation for an attack on Cerasola.

17th September—The plan was for B squadron to support the 2nd Kings in their attack on Point 137 and for C squadron and the 2nd-4th Hamps to clear Cerasola which was holding up the whole divisional front. At 0430 hours Lieut. B. E. S. King and

No. 1 troop of B squadron moved along the road to clear the area of Point 126.

Three machine-gun posts were cleared up by the 2nd Kings and Lieut King, although wounded, took his troop up to Point 137 by first light. He was being covered by No. 2 troop. Just after first light two of Lieut. King's tanks were knocked out by a German Mark IV tank from Point 126. This Mark IV was, in turn, quickly knocked out by No. 2 troop from their covering position. For the rest of the day, in very heavy shelling, Lieut. King made repeated trips to an observation post to direct artillery fire. Sjt. J. Maxwell and L.-Cpl. Gifford were wounded and Tpr. D. James was killed.

Meanwhile, on the left, C squadron started at 0530 hours and, guided by Lieut. Bexon, crossed the wadi in front of Cerasola and were on their objectives with the 2nd-4th Hamps by first light. Nos. 1 and 4 troops covered the left and No. 2 troop the right. All troops were heavily shelled and there was sniping from the houses at La Pastoro which the infantry could not get at to clear.

Lieut. A. N. MacCleary on the extreme left acted as observation post for the Royal Devon Yeomanry battery on several good shoots. At last light C squadron remained with the 2nd-4th Hamps until relieved by the Yorkshire Dragoons at 0200 hours.

18th September—During the previous afternoon A squadron had moved to Ospedaletto in preparation for the crossing of the river Aussa. They were to support the 1st Royal West Kents in this operation and were under command of the 12th Infantry Brigade.

The night of 17th-18th September was very confused, as the 1st Royal West Kents did not find the Cerasola ridge clear. Another attack by the Black Watch was also in progress on the right to clear the high ground overlooking the Aussa for an attack by the 51st Battalion Royal Tank Regiment.

At 0500 hours Major R. J. Griffiths, M.C., was still standing by as there was no firm bridgehead but he decided he must go before first light. Capt. A. K. E. Finch Noyes put out guides on the forward slope and No. 2 troop went down to look for a crossing. This proved easier than expected and Nos. 2 and 4 troops were quickly across, married up and supported their respective infantry companies on to their objectives, taking in all about 60 prisoners.

This operation was remarkably successful considering no reconnaissance had been made and a lot of it was done in the dark under heavy shelling. Both Lieut. F. A. Norris and Lieut. W. A. L. Reid deserve full credit. Again the tanks remained with the infantry throughout a very trying day.

19th September—The regiment remained in the Poggio area whilst Nos. 2 and 3 troops of A squadron relieved Nos. 1 and 4 troops, who were still with the 1st Royal West Kents bridgehead.

20th September—The A squadron troops were again relieved whilst B squadron moved to an area south of San Aquilina and

C squadron married up with the Royal Fusiliers of the 12th Infantry Brigade, but the operation was subsequently cancelled.

21st September—Heavy rain fell during the day and all squadrons were bogged down. The infantry made the high ground round Vergiano which they found unoccupied.

22nd September—B squadron moved to Vergiano in the afternoon. Under cover of a smoke screen Nos. 2 and 4 troops under Capt. R. S. H. Sidebottom crossed the river Marecchia just before last light and made a strong point in San Giustina with the Somerset Light Infantry. They were subjected to heavy shelling.

No. 2 troop of C squadron with Capt. C. M. Thomas, M.C., and Lieut. H E. Irwin's reconnaissance troop Shermans supported B squadron's crossing. They also had several good shoots into the valley round Sant' Arcangelo.

23rd September—B squadron had to send Nos. 1 and 5 troops to support the 2nd-4th Hamps in the Bornacino area at first light. This area, and San Giustina, was very heavily shelled all morning. At the same time the 5th Canadian Armoured Division was passing through but were having trouble from Sant' Arcangelo.

A squadron relieved Nos. 2 and 4 troops of B squadron at last light.

24th September—Nos. 1 and 3 troops of B squadron were relieved at last light by Lieut. H. E. Irwin, M.C., and No. 1 Troop of A squadron and this force was eventually relieved at 1930 hours the following day.

26th September—The regiment concentrated in the area of San Aquilina for re-fitting and resting, ready to move C squadron on the 30th September under command of the 25th Indian Infantry Brigade of the 10th Infantry Division.

Our hopes for rest and maintenance were denied us. We did, however, manage to get all the fighting troops away for forty-eight hours' leave and managed to get a certain amount of repair work carried out on the tanks.

SOGLIANO—MONTE FARNETO—CESENA

On 26th September the regiment had been ordered to be ready to support the 10th Indian Division, who were to take over from the 4th Indian Division on 1st October. The regiment alone supported the Division through October. The Division was four brigades strong and this meant very hard work for the three fighting squadrons since, at the best, it meant one squadron supporting a brigade.

The divisional line of advance was through the foothills of the main Apennine range flanking the main Rimini-Bologna road, the country being a series of steep ridges which ran across the line of advance. There was a steep wadi or river between each ridge. Each of these ridges had to be assaulted and by this movement, through very difficult country, the main defences on the Bologna road up to and including Cesena, were turned.

A very heavy burden was placed on squadron leaders and reconnaissance captains during this period, as every move had to be reconnoitred on foot. This also meant that tank commanders were constantly out of their tanks and up with the forward infantry trying to get their tanks into position. Enemy shell fire, due to good observation, was always accurate and heavy. We had two very severe losses during the period—Lieut.-Col. The Lord O'Neill and Major W. M. Mackean, M.C., both being killed whilst on reconnaissance.

Supply was also a major problem, but due to untiring work by squadron echelons and Headquarters squadron the forward tanks were reached every night.

2nd October—C squadron were under command of 25th Indian Infantry Brigade and were ordered to cross the Rubicon and relieve the 6th Battalion R. Tanks. By evening the squadron was concentrated in the area Cormacchiara and liaison established with the infantry. There was some shelling due to movement by the relieving troops. Heavy rain slowed up movement.

4th October—Lieut. Hubbard and No. 2 Troop moved up to Borghi during the day and a plan was made to attack S. Martino that night, using the 1st King's Own from the Montale direction. No. 2 troop was to support by fire on fixed lines. Good results were obtained according to the infantry but even with artificial moonlight shooting accurately was very difficult. The King's Own attack failed and at first light they were held on the edge of the village.

A and B squadrons moved into the Poggio Berni area.

5th October—During the previous day Major R. J. Griffith, M.C., had tied up with 20th Indian Infantry Brigade and during the night 4th-5th October Capt. A. K. E. Finch Noyes marched from Scorticata to the top of San Giovanni with a No. 22 wireless set on a mule, to keep in touch with the 2nd-3rd Royal Gurkhas who were directed on Sogliano. Lieut. J. A. Waters with No. 3 troop of A squadron, supported by Lieut. H. E. Irwin's Reconnaissance Troop Shermans, was to work round by road through Montale-Montevecchia in support. After the heavy rain the tanks were completely road-bound and when the leading tank was blown up on a mine they were unable to proceed. They were in view from San Martino and were heavily shelled. Meanwhile the 2nd-3rd Gurkhas captured Sogliano.

C squadron had been planning with the 1st King's Own during the day for another attack on San Martino. This was made during the night 5th-6th October and supported by Lieut. Bexon with No. 4 troop, C squadron, from Vecchiano, and by Lieut. Irwin's Shermans. The attack was very successful and by first light the village was clear.

The mined tank of A squadron was very ably recovered during the night by L-Sjt. Jackson and A squadron armoured recovery vehicle.

6th October—We now held the whole ridge from Sogliano to Borghi and plans were made for 20th Indian Infantry Brigade to capture Monte Farneto, supported by B squadron and for 25th Indian Infantry Brigade to capture Roncofreddo-San Lorenzo, supported by C squadron : A squadron sending No. 4 Troop under Lieut. J. S. Milne to Strigara, under command of the Central Indian Horse.

7th-8th October—On the night 6th-7th October reconnaissances of the river Fiumicino were carried out by both B and C squadrons. On B squadron's front the bridge below Sogliano was found intact and siezed, which simplified their problem. Lieut. MacCleary, Sjt. Williams and Sjt. Thacker all took out patrols for C squadron but could find no very suitable place as all the tracks down were narrow and steep. Lieut. MacCleary went out again on the night 7th-8th October and crossed the river, finding a possible place.

On the 7th October B squadron moved off before first light to support 20th Indian Infantry Brigade in the Monte Farneto attack. Major Mackean split the squadron and, with No. 2 troop and Lieut. Irwin's Shermans, was to help the 2nd-3rd Gurkhas on the right of the feature. Capt. Sidebottom, with Nos. 4 and 5 troops, was to support the 3rd Mahrattas on the left. Both battalions attacked with great dash and captured their objectives before first light. The tanks moved down a very winding road in the dark, led by Capt. Sidebottom, and over the bridge. It was now raining heavily and German fire was coming down. Capt. Sidebottom's force turned left, soon joined up with the 3rd Mahrattas, and took up counter-attack positions.

Major Mackean's force continued up the road but found the next culvert blown. There was no way round so he had to come back and go up the track used by Capt. Sidebottom. He eventually tied up with the 2nd-3rd Gurkhas at mid-day. At 1400 hours a very heavy counter-attack developed and Lieut. Irwin took his troop right up the east side and fired on Cidla Araldi where the attack was forming up. There were two more counter-attacks during the afternoon, both of which were beaten off. Shelling during the whole period was heavy and unfortunately Major Mackean was hit late in the afternoon and died in the regimental aid post. The tanks rallied for the night just behind the leading companies and were fully supplied and replenished by 0400 hours, Capt. Hern having a very warm time getting his jeeps and trailers through some heavy harassing fire.

8th October—It was still raining heavily. B squadron moved to counter-attack positions before first light and Lieut. Fleming took his troop up the east side. There were two counter-attacks and heavy shelling throughout the day.

C squadron moved off at 0300 hours in thick mist and rain with the intention of being on the infantry objectives by first light. The plan was—on the right : 3rd-18th Garhwals supported by Nos. 1 and 2 troops under Major R. D. Morton with objective San Lorenzo. On the left : 3rd-1st Punjabs supported by Nos. 3 and 4 troops under Capt. C. M. Thomas, M.C., with objective right of Roncofreddo. The going, owing to the heavy rain, was impossible and by 0700 hours it was obvious that the tanks could go no further, several being already badly bogged. The infantry were on their objectives by mid-day. Trooper G. King, a fitter, was killed by shellfire during the morning.

9th October—B squadron, still in counter-attack role on Monte Farneto, beat off another counter-attack and were subjected to heavy shelling.

C squadron were trying to get out of their bog, one tank being completely under water. Supply to both B and C squadrons was difficult, but jeeps and trailers proved invaluable. C squadron rations had to be floated across the river to them. Shelling was lighter.

10th October—Shelling on B squadron was still heavy but lighter elsewhere. C squadron extracted some tanks from the mud on to the San Lorenzo road. During the night, 10th-11th October, A squadron moved up to the area Sogliano.

11th October—The 10th Indian Infantry Brigade were now ordered to push on through 20th Indian Infantry Brigade. A squadron moved Nos. 2 and 3 troops in support of the 1st Durham Light Infantry, whose objective was Monteleone. Again the tanks were completely road-bound and had to advance through the small village of San Paola. This village was found still to contain some enemy but good shooting by No. 2 troop helped the 2nd-4th Gurkhas to clear it. This action also helped the Durhams. The road between San Paola and Monteleone was found to be mined so the two troops took up positions there.

B squadron were still on Monte Farneto and C squadron were re-organising in Roncofreddo.

12th-13th October—No movement was possible due to rain.

14th October—C squadron moved just east of Roncofreddo.

B squadron came under command of 10th Indian Infantry Brigade and moved to the area of Monteleone.

A squadron moved Nos. 2 and 3 troops to Sorrivoli in support of the 4th Baluchs. The track from San Paola to Sorrivoli was scarcely " jeepable " and due to the heavy rain no more tank moves were permitted.

15th October—Nos 2 and 3 troops, A squadron, under Lieut. W. A. L. Reid, and now reduced to three runners, tried to move from Sorrivoli to Dio La Guardia but were unable to reach the top due to the narrowness of the track and a blow. Engineers were called for and worked all night.

16th October—At 1300 hours the three tanks managed to reach the few buildings at Dio La Guardia, but progress was very slow and all had to have Royal Engineers' assistance A small bulldozer was giving great help. No. 2 troop, B squadron, tried to get up to Ardiano but got bogged.

17th October—Lieut. Reid got his A squadron tanks down to Monte Reale by first light and linked up with the 4th Baluchs. Any movement on this forward slope during daylight was heavily shelled.

18th October—Nearly all troop leaders in the regiment were out looking for ways forward as all movement of tanks on maintenance routes was disastrous. Lieut. Reid again got forward with his infantry to Aquarola, where they were shelled heavily all day.

19th October—A squadron were now overlooking the river Savio and reconnaissances were carried out to find a crossing. A possible place was found near Castiglione on Route 71. The Division was now forced to switch its maintenance route down the Sogliano-Mercato road and then up Route 71.

20th October—Reconnaissances were made of the river Savio. A ford below Mario Riopetra was found by Lieut. Milne, No. 4 troop, A squadron, who was with the Central Indian Horse.

21st October—C squadron moved from Roncofreddo to Cello via Mario Riopetra. Rain again poured down but all tanks were safely across the Savio before it rose. Tracks were in a terrible state.

The road forward from Cello to Borello was impassable, so the river bed was reconnoitred by Lieut. Milne and found to be just possible. The plan was for 20th Indian Infantry Brigade to attack Monte Cavallo supported by C squadron, and 25th Indian Infantry Brigade to attack Monte Della Rovere supported by A squadron. The attack went in on the night of the 21st and was only partially successful on 20th Brigade front. 25th Brigade and A squadron established only a small bridgehead. By the afternoon all of C squadron had got to Borello—a very good effort, Lieut. Milne walking all the way, sometimes up to his chest in water.

23rd October—B squadron moved from Monte Farneto to Borello to take over C squadron commitments with 20th Indian Infantry Brigade. C squadron were put under command of the 43rd Lorried Gurkha Brigade and were directed to Della Rovere. C squadron again moved down the river bed to Castiglione and so found the blows in Route 71. They then tried to get up the road but met two large demolitions. Meanwhile No. 4 troop, C squadron, went up the Monte Cavallo road in an effort to get across by the track from Monte Cavallo to Tesselo but were also held up by mines and blows. Engineers were put on both roads, our own section with the main part of C squadron, and did very valuable work. Lieut. Bexon and a serjeant from No. 4 troop, C squadron, went out during the night to look at the Tesselo track : it looked very doubtful.

24th October—The 43rd Lorried Gurkha Brigade attacked Tesselo with great success. C squadron made slow progress up the road to help them and Lieut. Bexon took No. 4 Troop down the track he had reconnoitred the night before. It was very bad and he took fifteen hours to do about one mile, but at last light reached the road Della Rovere where he was re-fuelled by Honeys which had followed him down.

B squadron pushed up the Monte Cavallo road to support the 3rd Mahrattas who were held up outside Teodorano. A plan was made by Major Sidebottom and the company commander, and No. 4 troop with a platoon of infantry reached Ardiano with No. 5 troop in support. There was heavy shelling and the Commanding Officer—Lieut. Colonel The Lord O'Neill—was killed and Major Sidebottom wounded. The tanks stayed till last light and then withdrew with the infantry.

25th October—The 1st-3rd Punjabs attacked Teodorano during the night and were successful. B squadron pushed down and were with them at first light. They then tried to push on towards Monte Palareto but were stopped by an impassable hogsback bridge.

C squadron spent a very trying day getting from Della Rovere to Polenta. Engineers had to work the whole way. There were eight different sorts of mines in one mile of road. The leading tank was blown up early on and the co-driver evacuated.

Supply was now a real problem ; B squadron could be reached by jeeps but C squadron were not reached for two days. The infantry supplies were on mules, the jeep-head being about five miles from the leading companies.

26th October—B squadron stuck in Teodorano and C squadron in the same position in Polenta. Reconnaissances of the river Ronco were carried out but division would not allow any tanks to move.

27th October—Further reconnaissance was carried out but no move was allowed.

29th October—The regiment was ordered to concentrate in the Cesena area.

FORLI.

REGIMENTAL HQ.

Leut.-Colonel. A. W. A. Llewellen-Palmer, D.S.O., M.C.,
Commandinr Officer.

Major P. Welch, M.C. ..	..	.. Second-in-Command
Capt. M. B. Pope, M.C. ..	..	.. Adjutant
Capt. J. B. Behr ..	..	.. Liaison Officer
Capt. R. B. M. King, M.C.	..	.. Signals Officer
Lieut. J. Maxwell ..	..	.. Intelligence Officer

Sjt. Hamilton
Sjt. Irvine
Cpl. Cox
Cpl. Keenan
Cpl. Reaks
Cpl. Murray
L/Cpl. Plenderleith
L/Cpl. McComish
Tpr. Allen
Tpr. Ging
Tpr. Kennedy
Tpr. Lyttle
Tpr. Beveridge
Tpr. O'Regan

Tpr. Smith
Tpr. Prince
Tpr. Sherer
Tpr. Horrocks
Tpr. Gothorp
Tpr. Wray
Tpr. Noble
Tpr. Hamilton, W.
Tpr. Templeton
Tpr. Godden
Tpr. Connolly
Tpr. McWilliams
Pte. Crothers, A.C.C.

MEDICAL GROUP
Captain B. Lush,
R.A.M.C.
Cpl. Gleghorne
Tpr. Higgins
Tpr. Holden
Tpr. Strong
Tpr. Chapman

ORDER OF BATTLE

" A " SQUADRON

H.Q. TROOP	No. 1 TROOP	No. 2 TROOP
Major Griffiths, M.C.	Lieut. Mahony	Lieut. Reid
Sjt. Mitchell	Tpr. Lees	L/Cpl. Ham, M.M.
L/Cpl. Graham, A.	Tpr. Martin, M.M.	Tpr. Harrison
L/Cpl. Brown	L/Cpl. Crisp	Tpr. Ranger
Tpr. Lynas	Tpr. Cameron	Tpr. Hines
	Sjt. Donaghy	Sjt. Barbour
	Tpr. Sartin	L/Cpl. Moore, T.
	Tpr. Reay	Tpr. Wesley
	Tpr. Cree	Tpr. Whyte
	Tpr. Tobias	Tpr. Hines
	Cpl. Stewart	
	Tpr. Tyndall	
	Tpr. Barr	
	L/Cpl. Ainsworth	
	Tpr. Tobias	

No. 3 Troop	No. 4 Troop
Lieut. Maguire, M.M.	Lieut. Milne
Tpr. Willman	Tpr. Cassells
Tpr. Smith	Tpr. Rees
Tpr. Young	Tpr. Lang
Tpr. Stokes, A.	Tpr. Stokes, B.
Sjt. Graham	Sjt. McIlherene
Tpr. Hodson	Tpr. Grey
Tpr. Walker	L/Cpl. Robinson
Tpr. Parker	Tpr. Gledhill
Tpr. Calland	Tpr. Lee
Cpl. Hutchman	Cpl. McFarland
Tpr. Donaldson	Tpr. Farmer
Tpr. McConnell	L/Cpl. Conroy
Tpr. McWilliams	Tpr. Gregory
Tpr. Taggart	Tpr. Hughes

RELIEFS AND SPARE CREWS

Sjt. Young	Cpl. Fallis	L/Cpl. Johnston, M.M.
L/Cpl. Harris	Tpr. Howard	Tpr. Patrick
Tpr. Peden	Tpr. Rees	Tpr. Conroy
Tpr. Gregory	Tpr. Lang	Tpr. Harrison, E.
Sjt. Smith, G.C.	Tpr. Harding	Tpr. Hancher
L/Cpl. Sherritt		Tpr. Lymer

VEHICLE MECHANICS' ECHELON

A.R.V. CREW	HALF-TRACK	
L/Sjt. Jackson	Sjt. Trotter	S/Sjt. Derrick, R.E.M.E.
Tpr. Bailey	Cpl. Duffin	Tpr. Sherlock
Tpr. Gallaher	Tpr. Eyre	Tpr. Meichen
Tpr. Hawkridge	Tpr. Howat	L/Cpl. Lockhart
Cfn. Mattick, R.E.M.E.		

" A " SQUADRON ECHELON

Capt. R. H. Bowring

S.Q.M.S. Allen	Tpr. Duncan
Sjt. Baird	Tpr. Eekins
Sjt. Moore	Tpr. Henderson
Cpl. Baker	Tpr. Kane
Cpl. Haren	Tpr. Lissaman
Cpl. Lyne	Tpr. Malcolmson
Cpl. Lavery	Tpr. Mann
L/Cpl. Cunningham	Tpr. Morrison
L/Cpl. Cox, R.	Tpr. Morris
L/Cpl. Graham, D. C.	Tpr. Mitchell
L/Cpl. McKillen	Tpr. McLaughlin
L.U.L.C. Marshall	Tpr. McCombe
L.U.L.C. Patton	Tpr. Richmond
Tpr. Armstrong	Tpr. Reynolds
Tpr. Coyle	Tpr. Sterritt
Tpr. Cunningham	Tpr. Wells
Tpr. Wardle	Tpr. Williams
Tpr. Wesley, H.	Tpr. Ward

COOKS		FITTERS
Cpl. Boyle		Cpl. McIntosh
L.U.L.C. Griffiths		Tpr. Barlow
Pte. Chartres		Tpr. Barnacle
Pte. Flynn		

JEEP		SCOUT CAR
Tpr. Mann		Capt. King
L/Cpl. Graham, D.		Tpr. Bell

" B " SQUADRON

H.Q. TROOP	No. 1 TROOP	No. 2 TROOP
Major Finch Noyes	Lieut. King, M.C.	Lieut. Fleming
Cpl. Chester	Tpr. Johnston, A.	Tpr. Knott
L/Cpl. Hughes	Tpr. Gray	L/Cpl. Martin, T.
Cpl. Hayward	Tpr. Buxton	L/Cpl. Gault
Tpr. Bowers	Tpr. O'Keefe	Tpr. Jennings
Sjt. Burns	Sjt. Bullick	Sjt. McAughtry
Tpr. Stafford	Tpr. McKinney	Tpr. Walker, E.
Tpr. Wood	Tpr. Moore, H. J.	Tpr. Kerr
Tpr. Dalzell	Tpr. Robinson, A.	Tpr. Ibbotson
Tpr. Symonds	Tpr. Fuller	Tpr. Richards
Cpl. McCullough	Cpl. Wheatley	Cpl. Wiggins
Tpr. Sharples	Tpr. Coppin	Tpr. Harrow
Tpr. Johnston, J.	Tpr. Bishop	Tpr. Rexworthy
L/Cpl. Collard	Tpr. Chilton	Tpr. Cawley
Tpr. Dawson, N. H.	Tpr. Bateson	Tpr. Hanson

No. 4 TROOP	No. 5 TROOP
Lieut. Foott	Lieut. Mahon
Tpr. Jeffrey	Tpr. Hamilton
Tpr. Dawson, R.	Tpr. McClurg
L/Cpl. Giboney	L./Cpl. Wallace
Tpr. Holt	Tpr. Corbin
Sjt. Wolfe	Sjt. Cheater
L/Cpl. Fennell	Tpr. Macartney
Tpr. Glass	Tpr. Gardiner
Tpr. Shanks	Tpr. Gomm
Tpr. Fitzgerald	
Cpl. Malseed	Sjt. Verso
Tpr. Webb	Tpr. Parker
Tpr. Warner	Tpr. Newman
Tpr. Perkins	L/Cpl. Binstead
Tpr. Doupe	Tpr. Smith, A. G.

FORWARD ECHELON

FITTERS	A.R.V. CREW
Sjt. Holmes	L/Cpl. Hughes
Cpl. Day	L/Cpl. Beatty
Tpr. Brindle	Tpr. Handley
L/Cpl. Wallace	Tpr. Gilligan
L/Cpl. Russell	Tpr. Donaghy

SCOUT CAR	JEEP
Tpr. Griffiths	Tpr. Grant, W.

" B " SQUADRON ECHELON
Capt. W. R. Hern

S.S.M. Humston	Tpr. Fell
S.Q.M.S. Burke	Tpr. Wilson
Sjt. Fleming	Tpr. Fletcher
Cpl. Nelson	Tpr. Mollan
Cpl. Crealey	Tpr. Bourne
Cpl. Graham	Tpr. Clarke
Cpl. Lowry	Tpr. Robinson
Cpl. McKenzie	Tpr. Thompson
L/Cpl. Gaston	Tpr. Pilsworth
L/Cpl. Duckers	Tpr. Saunderson
L/Cpl. Miller	Tpr. Higgins
L/Cpl. Dunlop	Tpr. Allen
Tpr. Vance	Tpr. Cantillon
Tpr. McIlveen	Tpr. White, J.
Tpr. Hassard	Tpr. Moffatt
Tpr. Greenfield	Tpr. Ceirans
Tpr. White, J. A.	Tpr. Waterson

FITTERS	COOKS
Cpl. Baillie	Cpl. Stevenson
Tpr. Andews	Pte. Jameson
Tpr. Cogran	Pte. Murray
	Pte. Spiers

" C " SQUADRON

H.Q. TROOP	No. 1 TROOP	No. 2 TROOP
Major Morton, M.C.	Lieut. Cumming	Lieut. Hubbard
L/Cpl. Pollard	L/Cpl. Gregson	Tpr. Warnock
Tpr. Bateson	Tpr. McAloon	Tpr. Smithdale
L/Cpl. Wilson, F.	L/Cpl. Walker	L/Cpl. James
Tpr. Gray, E.	Tpr. Warrender	Tpr. Sibley
Lieut. A. N. MacCleary	L/Sjt. Coxhill	L/Sjt. Shaw
L/Cpl. Boyd, T. A.	Tpr. McGrath	Tpr. Lodge
—	Tpr. Robertson	Tpr. Evans
—	L/Cpl. Winyard	Tpr. Rodgers
—	Tpr. Millson	Tpr. Nolan
		Tpr. Harvey
		L/Cpl. Neill
		Tpr. O'Neill

No. 3 TROOP	No. 4 TROOP	RELIEFS
Sjt. Kennedy, M.M.	Lieut. Corrie	Cpl. Ackroyd
Tpr. Lambie	Tpr. Cooper	Tpr. Morrison
Tpr. Clegg	Tpr. Griffin	Tpr. Parfitt
Tpr. Richardson	Cpl. Hamilton	L/Cpl. Jefferson
Tpr. Cockerill	Tpr. Burton, S.	
Sjt. Christie	Sjt. Baker	
Tpr. Aldridge, K.	Tpr. Harper, R.	
Tpr. Fort, A.	Tpr. Wardle	
Tpr. Derbyshire	Tpr. Hellawell	
Tpr. Holmes		

COMPOSITE SQUADRON

Lieut. Corrie
Tpr. Dyer
Tpr. Smithdale
L/Cpl. James
Tpr. Yates

Sjt. Garrigan, M.M.
L/Cpl. Peters
Tpr. Parfitt
L/Cpl. Walker
Tpr. Eastwood

Sjt. Bell
Tpr. Morrison

L/Cpl. Jefferson
Tpr. Bigg

Cpl. Cunningham
Cpl. Sloan
Tpr. Prince, C.
L/Cpl. Dougall
L/Cpl. Cowan

FITTERS

Sjt. Gettings, R.
Cpl. McAteer
Tpr. McBay

L/Sjt. Stewart, J.
Tpr. Hill
Tpr. Martin

Cpl. Mogey
Tpr. Davis
Tpr. Lusty

SUPPLY ECHELON

S.S.M. Bumstead
Tpr. McNeill
Tpr. Hamilton
Tpr. Chartres

Sjt. Murray
Tpr. Darragh
Tpr. L'Clery
Tpr. McDowell

L/Cpl. Dixon
Tpr. McQuilkin
Tpr. Bishop
Tpr. Scott

H.Q. SQUADRON

TANK AND SCOUT CAR CREWS

Capt. H. E. Irwin, M.C.
Sjt. Phillips
Sjt. Lytle
Cpl. Lester
L/Cpl. Duke
Tpr. Robinson, S.
Tpr. Critchley
L/Cpl. Taylor, F.
L/Cpl. Brown, J.
Tpr. Mooney
Tpr. Andrewan
Tpr. Anderson, C.
Tpr. Lang
Tpr. Hanna, J.
Tpr. Wilson, J.

Cpl. Greene
L/Cpl. Simpson
Tpr. Creedon
Tpr. Campbell, S.
Tpr. Mavitty
Tpr. Bitchenor

L/Cpl. Casey
L/Cpl. Dougall
L/Cpl. Greenwood
Tpr. Steel
Tpr. Hazelton
Tpr. Miller
Tpr. Taylor
Tpr. Burrows
Tpr. Houlton
Tpr. Morris

Lieut. E. D. Bullick
Sjt. Craig, L.D.M.
Sjt. Wingfield
Cpl. Patterson
Cpl. Brown, H.
L/Cpl. Hadley
L/Cpl. Cannell
Tpr. Bane
Tpr. Dawson, R.
Tpr. Whitehurst
Tpr. Field
Tpr. Harrison, S.
Tpr. Small, S.
Tpr. McCann
Tpr. Smith
Tpr. Creighton
Tpr. McGrath
Tpr. Taylor, L.
Tpr. Snowden

Sjt. Smyth
Cpl. Marsh
Cpl. Rogers
Cpl. Beal
Tpr. Anderson, F.
Tpr. Catton
Tpr. Fisher

Tpr. Humphries
Tpr. Askew
Tpr. Day

FITTERS
Cpl. Johnson, A.
Tpr. Fuller
Tpr. Murphy
Tpr. Andrew

H.Q. SQUADRON ECHELON

Major W. G. Lavery
R.S.M. Fidler
R.Q.M.S. Docksey
S.S.M. Fowler
Sjt. McWilliams
Sjt. Moorhead
Sjt. McGahey
Sjt. McDonagh
Cpl. Cawley
Cpl. Dunlop
Cpl. Pollitt
Cpl. Rocke, S.
Cpl. Stewart, D.
L/Cpl. Cassidy
L/Cpl. Henderson
L/Cpl. Sutherland
L/Cpl. Garner
L/Cpl. Bogle
L/Cpl. Brownlee, J.
L/Cpl. Dermott
L/Cpl. Moore, R.
Tpr. Armstrong, K.
Tpr. Atkinson
Tpr. Andrew
Tpr. Brookes
Tpr. Bott
Tpr. Brenan
Tpr. Copp
Tpr. Dann
Tpr. Donaghy
Tpr. Ferguson

Capt. E. S. Robinson
Tpr. Furphy
Tpr. Fiddes
Tpr. Graham
Tpr. Gray
Tpr. Hanna, D.
Tpr. Hawkins
Tpr. Johnson
Tpr. Kennewell
Tpr. Laverty
Tpr. Logue
Tpr. Latimer
Tpr. Lennon
Tpr. Magee
Tpr. McDowell, W.
Tpr. McDonald, D.
Tpr. Morton
Tpr. McDowell, J.
Tpr. Morris
Tpr. Purvis
Tpr. Reynolds
Tpr. Robertson
Tpr. Shipton
Tpr. Smalley
Tpr. Vennard
Tpr. Wylie
Tpr. Young
Tpr. Knopp
Tpr. Broadhurst
Tpr. Moonan

Q.M.S. (M.) Vanstone, C.
Sjt. Whyte, A.
Cpl. Marsh
Tpr. Steele
Tpr. Thompson, C.
Tpr. Dickenson

Q.M.S.(T.) Scott, E.
Sjt. Smith, R. A. D.
Cpl. Abbott
L/Cpl. Abbott
L/Cpl. Reid
Tpr. Harwood
Tpr. Allard
Tpr. Smith, W.

Sjt. Walford
Tpr. Fletcher
Tpr. Hodge
Tpr. Fuller, C.

L/Cpl. Toombes, S.
Tpr. Hart
Tpr. Dann

COOKS
Cpl. McKee
Pte. Evans
Pte. Hitchcock

It was expected that the regiment would remain in Cesena for approximately sixteen days' rest and re-fit. A workshops' programme was arranged and many officers and other ranks sent on a well-earned leave. Great difficulty was experienced in arranging the concentration as both B and C squadrons were stuck in the hills around Monte Cavallo due to the heavy rain. However, by the 3rd of November the last B squadron tank was back in Cesena.

7th November—Brigadier J. N. Tetley, D.S.O., T.D., Commander of 25th Army Tank Brigade, arrived and ordered a composite squadron to be formed immediately to support the 12th Infantry Brigade of 4th British Infantry Division. This squadron was formed with difficulty due to leave and overhauls.

Lieut.-Colonel A. W. A. Llewellen-Palmer, D.S.O., M.C., arrived and assumed command of the regiment.

The fighting from the 9th November until the 3rd December is difficult to follow without a large-scale map. The operations consisted of the clearing of Forli, the crossing of the Montone and approaches to the Lamone rivers. Incessant rain made movement off the road almost impossible. The country here is absolutely flat except for the flood banks, is very highly cultivated with vines growing on poplar trees in rows about fifty feet apart. It is intersected by canals which, at this time of year, are full of water and complete tank obstacles. There are farmhouses and buildings every few hundred yards. This meant house-to-house fighting all the way. The enemy fought for every yard of ground and a day's fighting seldom resulted in more than a few hundred yards advance. No outflanking was possible. The enemy had more infantry on the ground than we had and every road was covered by enemy tanks or anti-tank guns. These had to be spotted, then made to move by our own fire or by heavy artillery or, weather permitting—which it seldom did—by fighter-bombers.

The regiment supported eight different brigades in this short period. As one infantry brigade became exhausted it was relieved by another to whom we transferred. In the end the regiment was reduced to four operational tanks. We were short of tanks all the time as we started operations in the middle of a complete overhaul and engine change. Tanks came up from workshops in one's and two's, thus orders of battle for this period altered constantly.

The methods used to deal with enemy-held buildings varied considerably. The most usual was for one tank to go forward and engage at point-blank range, covered by the second tank—on a pre-arranged signal the infantry rushed the house. The remaining Germans then usually surrendered. Sometimes the infantry led, covered by the fire from tanks. The capture of each house, ditch or canal had to have a separate plan.

8th November—The composite squadron moved to Forlimpopoli at 0700 hours and remained there the rest of the day. The force then split as under :—

With 6th Black Watch (6th B.W.)—Major R. J. Griffiths, M C., and two troops of A squadron.

With 4th Royal West Kents (4th R.W.K.)—Capt. H. E. Irwin, M.C., and remainder of force (three troops). Their task was to support their two battalions in an attack across the airfield to sieze Forli. The airfield and bridgehead over the Ronco river had already been cleared and formed by 28th Infantry Brigade and 10th Infantry Brigade respectively.

9th November—The squadron moved off at 0001 hours from Forlimpopoli. The route was very difficult to follow due to mist, but had been reconnoitred by Capt. Irwin who got the column safely to the airfield. Further reconnaissance had then to be made to contact the two battalions, as visibility was about five yards.

By first light both Major Griffith and Capt. Irwin were linked up with their infantry. Major Griffith's force moved forward with the leading company of the Black Watch and No. 1 troop was soon up to Route 9 where there was a blow. Meanwhile Capt. Irwin's leading troop was badly held up trying to follow his battalion. It was soon apparent that the enemy had withdrawn and with good help from the Black Watch Pioneers, Major Griffith was soon in Forli. Capt. Irwin followed Major Griffith in.

At mid-day No. 1 troop had to go to the help of the leading company of the Black Watch who were held up on the northern outskirts of the town. Lieut. Mahony shot up all the houses indicated, but the company was unable to get forward. Capt. Irwin's force and the R.W.K. consolidated.

Regimental headquarters moved into Forli.

10th November—No. 2 troop, A squadron, moved up to support the leading company of the Black Watch at first light. The enemy position was stronger than anticipated. The commanding officer and Major Griffith made a plan and, using two Shermans in support, Lieut. Maguire took his troop in with a fresh company. The enemy fought very hard and every house had to be cleared. The troop fired all its own ammunition and the infantry reached their objectives, but the company commander was killed and they had about forty casualties, so the position was consolidated and Lieut. Maguire returned at last light. The enemy proved to be a company of Field Marshal Kesselring's Assault Battalion—all picked men. They were all killed except six, who were taken prisoner. For his gallant part in this action Sjt. J. Barbour of A squadron won the Military Medal.

Meanwhile, on the right, Capt. Irwin had been supporting the West Kents. The Royal Engineers were supposed to put in an Ark over a blow to enable him to get up. It was badly put in and it was not until mid-day that he was able to get up to the leading company. One tank of C squadron was " bazooka'd " with two casualties—Cpl. Cunningham and Tpr. Yates. The force had to remain for the night with the forward company. A half-squadron of the 142nd Regiment R.A.C. was put under command of N.I.H.

11th November—The half-squadron of 142nd Regiment R.A.C. with the Royal Fusiliers went through Capt. Irwin's force but did not make much progress.

The Black Watch consolidated.

12th November—Major Griffith took out his two troops to support the Black Watch who were trying to push forward to the river Montone. A fresh half-squadron of the 142nd Regiment R.A.C., with the Royal Fusiliers were on his right. No. 2 Troop got on well and reached their first objective with the leading company. No. 1 Troop (Serjeant Donaghy) then passed through but had only moved a few hundred yards when the air observation reported three enemy tanks at San Tome. Air and artillery were brought down, but, as usual, every house was held and some very hard fighting ensued. Major Griffith and the company commander had to make a plan to get every house. The force remained with the infantry for the night. Sjt. Donaghy's tank was blown up on multiple mines in the late afternoon and he was wounded. In spite of this Sjt. Donaghy recovered his tank under heavy fire. For his great work this day Sjt. Donaghy was awarded the Military Medal.

13th November—Another half-squadron was formed in Forli under Capt. R. H. Bowring, to support the West Kents. The big ditch beyond San Tome was crossed with a fascine and Lieut. J. S. Milne got up to the leading company and remained there for the night.

14th November—Capt. Bowring remained with the West Kents for a fairly quiet day except for shelling.

15th to 18th November—The regiment concentrated in Forli.

20th November—Two troops of C squadron moved to the area of Filetto to support the 4th-10th Baluch of 10th Indian Infantry Brigade.

21st November—The commanding officer and Major R. D. Morton, M.C., commanding A squadron, visited headquarters, 4th-10th Baluchs, under whose command C squadron were sent. The forward positions were some 200 to 300 yards from the bank of the river Montone, in houses, and the enemy were holding dug-out positions and houses on the river bank itself. The country was thick and cultivated and before the tanks could get into any sort of position a small canal had to be crossed which necessitated a fascine. Meanwhile a reconnaissance of the crossing was made and a likely place chosen. The remainder of C squadron arrived in harbour by 1700 hours.

23rd September—A fascine arrived early in the morning and was fixed to Sjt. Kennedy's tank by mid-day. A plan was made to clear houses near the river, as the first phase, with one platoon and to clear other houses on the bank as a second phase with two platoons. Unfortunately the fascine tank bogged but with the help of the infantry bundles of sticks were thrown into the canal and No. 4 troop went across and contacted the infantry. They successfully shot the platoon into the houses and pulled back to re-organise for the second objective but the light was rapidly fading so the commanding officer of the 4th-10th Baluch postponed the attack until the following morning.

24th November—Air support was called for and arrived in the morning, after night patrols had reported the enemy dug into the banks and using tunnels through the canal. The flood banks were about thirty feet high on both sides of the river. These banks were the only high ground in the Po Valley. The enemy dug deep into them and was immune from all forms of fire. The banks were complete tank obstacles in themselves and formed the basis of every German defensive line. This was the first of many we were to meet in the Po Valley. No better obstacle could be devised.

At 1430 hours No. 4 troop crossed the canal again and went in to deal with houses near the bank of the river Montone. All went well until the infantry reached the houses, then Spandau and heavy shelling forced them to ground. The fire was coming from the bank and opposite side of the river and the tanks found it impossible to locate them. Meanwhile No. 1 troop had crossed the canal and come up to support No. 4 Troop. · An enemy tank was spotted on the bank on the other side but disappeared before it could be engaged. The infantry commanding officer decided to withdraw but he had no communication with his leading platoon.

Lieut. G. C. Cumming got out of his tank and eventually found the platoon leader in one of the houses and told him to withdraw. No. 1 Troop covered their withdrawal and both troops came back to harbour for the night. The 4th-10th Baluch had suffered casualties and the commanding officer decided to give the position a rest.

Crocodiles were suggested as the ideal weapon and the commanding officer of N.I.H. managed to get two from the 142nd Regiment R.A.C., but owing to more rain they could not get up to the bank.

25th November—No. 2 troop shot up houses on the other side of the river during the morning. The forward observation officer of the Royal Devon Yeomanry knocked down the church tower in the village, which was being used as an enemy observation post.

C squadron concentrated in Filetto under command of the 43rd Lorried Gurkhas who relieved the 10th Indian Infantry Brigade in this sector.

26th November—B squadron moved through Forli at 0600 hours over the Bailey Bridge and made contact with the 1st Durham Light Infantry who had made a crossing during the night—on the far bank of the river Montone at Casa Boschi. Major A. K. E. Finch Noyes made his tactical headquarters at San Bermado. Thus the regiment had one squadron over the river and two squadrons on the east bank. The general plan was to clear up both banks of the Montone northwards to give 1st Canadian Division enough room and a good start for their coming attack to the Lamone. No. 2 troop shot up several houses but the opposition was stiff and a further plan necessary.

27th November—One company of the 2nd-4th Gurkhas, under command of the 1st Durham Light Infantry, were supported by No. 2 troop and further progress in clearing the bank was made. No. 5 Troop shelled houses.

28th November—B squadron remained in support of the 1st D.L.Is. A squadron were in reserve and C squadron with the 43rd Lorried Indian Brigade.

29th November—A squadron moved from Forli to Filetto area in support of the 2nd-4th Gurkhas. An attack was planned with B squadron and the 1st D.L.Is. on the left, with A squadron and the 2nd-4th Gurkhas on the right, to clear up more of the bank and its vicinity.

30th November—Lieut. E. D. Bullick got an Ark into position by 1115 hours and this enabled B squadron to get No. 2 troop up to B company of the 1st D. L. Is., and No. 5 troop in support of A company, who had filtered over the canal in the night. Both companies dug in and consolidated.

On the right A squadron moved Nos. 2 and 3 troops in support of the 2nd-4th Gurkhas ; No. 2 troop led and it was all road work—several prisoners being collected.

On reaching their objective, a cross-roads, No. 2 troop and C company consolidated but came under heavy shell fire. The battalion commander decided to continue straight on to the final objective with C company and No. 2 troop. On moving off again more prisoners were taken and track marks turning off the road were spotted by Lieut. W. A. L. Reid, No. 2 troop leader. He immediately engaged the houses on his left and " brewed up " a self-propelled gun. The crew of another were seen to bale out. Both guns were captured. The area was consolidated, but heavily shelled by the enemy. The tanks withdrew at last light to harbour, having completed their task and cleared both sides of the river for two thousand yards.

1st December—One troop of B squadron, consisting of one 95 mm. tank and one 6-pounder, moved up while No. 2 troop went back, remaining in position till last light to cover the take-over by the Royal 22nd Regiment of Canada.

During the night of 30th November-1st December the 4th-10th Baluch relieved the 2nd-4th Gurkhas. At approximately 1000 hours No. 1 Troop of A squadron, supporting C company, engaged some houses and these were taken by the infantry with little opposition.

No. 3 troop, in support of C company, advanced up the road, two prisoners being taken early on. Sixteen prisoners were taken further up this road in more house to house fighting. The leading tank moved off and remained in support in the area of Casa Palacci. The troop leader's tank moved to a road junction north west, together with the platoon. The houses further on were held in strength and it was decided to consolidate at Casa Palacci where the platoon dug in and the tanks were sited in defensive positions.

During this action No. 1 troop killed a number of enemy in the vineyards. About 1600 hours a counter-attack developed after shelling and mortaring. This was beaten off with the aid of artillery and aircraft.

At dusk the tanks thinned out, being finally withdrawn at 1900 hours and the infantry were relieved by the West Nova Scotia Regiment.

2nd December—The regiment received orders to remain in support of the Canadians until relieved by the 12th Battalion

Royal Tank Regiment. At 0900 hours No. 5 troop, B squadron, with A company of the Royal 22nd Regiment moved towards Prada, reaching it at 1005 hours. At 1055 hours they reached a road junction, and, while the tanks were engaging houses on the Russi road, Lieut. Mahon's and Sjt. Burns' tanks were hit by an anti-tank gun, casualties being four killed and two wounded. The killed were Sjt. Burns, Tpr. Corbin, Tpr. Stafford and Tpr. Wood ; wounded, L.-Cpl. Wallace and Tpr. McClurg. Sjt. Verso's tank was in position behind a house and was not hit. He gave support to the company when they were heavily counter-attacked. His was the only wireless set left with the leading company. This tank did the work of a troop and restored the situation. For his part in this action Sjt. Verso won the Military Medal.

No. 2 troop moved up but were not used. At last light both troops harboured in the area of Prada.

A squadron were ordered to support the West Nova Scotia Regiment in the advance towards the River Lamone and at 0915 hours Nos. 2 and 4 troops moved off with their infantry. Once again houses caused trouble. Four prisoners were taken, the remainder of the enemy being killed. The bridge was found to be blown and the Scolo Via Cupa proved impassable to tanks. One platoon of infantry succeeded in crossing and occupying the houses.

Enemy movement north of the Scolo Via Cupa was successfully engaged. A counter-attack developed about 1600 hours and another later. These were beaten off with the aid of artillery and the tanks. The tanks remained in support until the infantry reserve company got across, when they withdrew.

The regiment was relieved by the 12th Battalion Royal Tank Regiment and concentrated in Forli.

WINTER LINE

REGIMENTAL H.Q. ADMINISTRATIVE GROUP

Lieut.-Colonel A. W. A. Llewellen-Palmer, D.S.O., M.C.
Commanding Officer

Major P. Welch, M.C.	.. Second-in-Command
Capt. M. B. Pope, M.C.	.. Adjutant
Capt. J. B. Behr	.. Liaison Officer
Lieut. B. E. S. King, M.C. ..	.. Signals Officer
Lieut. W. A. Ingram	.. Intelligence Officer

Sjt. Hamilton
Sjt. Irvine
Cpl. Cox
Cpl. Keenan
Cpl. Murray
L/Cpl. Plenderleith
L/Cpl. McComish
Tpr. Allen
Tpr. Ging
Tpr. Kennedy
Tpr. Lyttle
Tpr. McIlveen
Tpr. O'Regan

Tpr. Smith
Tpr. Turnham
L/Cpl. Toombes

Tpr. Wray
Tpr. Noble
Tpr. Hamilton, W.
Tpr. Templeton
Tpr. Connolly
Tpr. Wylie
Tpr. Gothorp
Pte. Arnold, A.C.C.

MEDICAL GROUP

Captain B. Lush, succeeded by Captain P. L. Blaxter, R.A.M.C.
Cpl. Cleghorne
Tpr. Higgins
Tpr. Holden
Tpr. Strong
Tpr. Chapman

ORDER OF BATTLE

"A" SQUADRON

H.Q. Troop	No. 1 Troop	No. 2 Troop
Capt. King	Sjt. Smith	Lieut. Reid, M.C.
Sjt. Mitchell	Tpr. Lees	Tpr. Hodson
L/Cpl. Bainbridge	Tpr. Harding	Tpr. Hanshaw
Tpr. Patrick	L/Cpl. Crisp	L/Cpl. Miller
Tpr. Peden	Tpr. Harrison, E.	Tpr. Hancher
Lieut. Waters	Cpl. Burry	Sjt. Smith
Tpr. Tarbard	Tpr. Sartin	Tpr. Jacobs
Tpr. Cumming	Tpr. Reay	Tpr. Wesley
Tpr. Hawkridge	Tpr. Cree	Tpr. Whyte
Tpr. Allen	Tpr. Thompson	Tpr. McNally
Sjt. Young	Cpl. Stewart	Cpl. McKee
Tpr. Howard	Tpr. Tyndall	L/Cpl. Ham, M.M.
Tpr. Green	Tpr. Barr	Tpr. Harrison
L/Cpl. Brown	L/Cpl. Ainsworth	Tpr. Hines
Tpr. Lynas	Tpr. Tobias	Cpl. Lavery
Cpl. Fallis		
Tpr. Connor		
Tpr. Cowan		
L/Cpl. Johnston, M.M.		

No. 3 Troop	No. 4 Troop	Reliefs and Spare Crews
Lieut. Maguire, M.M.	Lieut. Knight, B.E.M.	Lieut. Milne
Tpr. Smith	Tpr. Cassells	Sjt. Smith
Tpr. Clarke	Tpr. Rees	L/Cpl. Harris
Tpr. Young	Tpr. Land	Tpr. Wills
Tpr. Stokes, A.	Tpr. Stokes, B.	Tpr. Morris-Francis
Cpl. Hutchman	Sjt. McIlherene	Lieut. Davis
Tpr. Donaldson	Tpr. Grey	Sjt. Perioli
Tpr. McConnell	L/Cpl. Robinson	Sjt. McIlherene
Tpr. McWilliams	Tpr. Gledhill	Tpr. Cameron
Tpr. Taggart	Tpr. Lymer	Tpr. Hines
L/Cpl. Moore	Cpl. McFarland	Sjt. Craig
L/Cpl. Church, M.M.	Tpr. McKinley	Cpl. Watson
Tpr. Walker	L/Cpl. Conroy	
Tpr. Parker	L/Cpl. Sherritt	
Tpr. Calland	Tpr. Hughes	

Jeep		Scout Car
Tpr. Mann		Capt. R. H. Bowring
		Tpr. Bell

FITTERS

A.R.V. Crew		Half-Track
L/Sjt. Jackson	Cpl. Duffin	S/Sjt. Derrick, R.E.M.E.
Tpr. Bailey	Tpr. Eyre	Tpr. Howat
Tpr. Gallaher	Tpr. Sherlock	Tpr. Meichen
Tpr. Hawkridge		
Cfn. Mattick, R.E.M.E.		

"A" SQUADRON ECHELON

S.S.M. Boon	Tpr. Eakins
S.Q.M.S. Allen	Tpr. Henderson
Sjt. Moore	Tpr. Kane
Cpl. Baker	Tpr. Lissaman
Cpl. Haren	Tpr. Malcolmson
Cpl. Lyne	Tpr. Morrison
Cpl. Lavery	Tpr. Mitchell
L/Cpl. Cunningham	Tpr. McLaughlin
L/Cpl. Cox, R.	Tpr. McCombe
L/Cpl. Graham, D.	Tpr. Richmond
L/Cpl. McKillen	Tpr. Reynolds
L.U.L.C. Marshall	Tpr. Sterritt
L.U.L.C. Patton	Tpr. Stevens
Tpr. Armstrong	Tpr. Wells
Tpr. Coyle	Tpr. Wardle
Tpr. Cunningham	Tpr. Wesley, H.
Tpr. Duncan	Tpr. Williams, J.
	Tpr. Ward

Fitters	Cooks
Cpl. McIntosh	Cpl. Boyle
L/Cpl. Lockhart	L.U.L.C. Griffiths
Tpr. Barlow	Pte. Chartres
Tpr. Barnacle	Pte. Flynn
	Pte. Hales
	Pte. Kelly

" B " SQUADRON

H.Q. Troop	No. 1 Troop	No. 2 Troop
Major Sidebottom	Lieut. Corrie	Sjt. McAughtry
Cpl. Chester	Tpr. Johnston	Tpr. Walker, E.
L/Cpl. Hughes	Tpr. Gray	Tpr. Kerr
L/Cpl. Gault	Tpr. Buxton	Tpr. Ibbotson
Tpr. Bowers	Tpr. O'Keefe	Tpr. Richards
Capt. Irwin	Sjt. Bullick	Cpl. Wiggins
Tpr. Sharples	Tpr. McKinney	Tpr. Harrow
Cpl. Keville	L/Cpl. Cox, C. A.	Tpr. Rexworthy
L/Cpl. Collard	Tpr. Moore, H. J.	Tpr. Cawley
Tpr. Dawson, N. H.	Tpr. Fuller	Tpr. Hanson
Sjt. McCullough	Cpl. Wheatley	L/Cpl. Martin
Cpl. Walls	Tpr. Coppin	Tpr. Ward
Tpr. Young	Tpr. Bishop	Tpr. Jennings
Tpr. Dalzell	Tpr. Chilton	Tpr. Shanks
Tpr. Johnston, J. B.	Tpr. Bateson	Tpr. Doupe

No. 4 Troop	No. 5 Troop
Lieut. Foott	Liuet. Bullick
L/Cpl. Gibboney	Tpr. Hamilton
Tpr. Dawson, R.	L/Cpl. Daville
L/Cpl. Moore	Tpr. Abbott
Tpr. Holt	Tpr. Brotton
Sjt. Wolfe	Sjt. Smith
L/Cpl. Fennell	Tpr. Gomm
Tpr. Glass	Tpr. Parker
Tpr. Fitzgerals	L/Cpl. Binstead
Tpr. Gamble	Tpr. Newman
Cpl. Malseed	Sjt. Cheter
Tpr. Webb	Tpr. Gardiner
Tpr. Jeffrey	Tpr. White, V. N.
Tpr. Perkins	Tpr. Symonds
Tpr. Warner	Tpr. Sumners

FORWARD ECHELON

Fitters	A.R.V. Crew
Sjt. Holmes	L/Cpl. Hughes
Cpl. Day	L/Cpl. Beatty
Tpr. Brindle	Tpr. Handley
L/Cpl. Wallace	Tpr. Gilligan
L/Cpl. Russell	Tpr. Donaghy

Scout Car	Jeep
Tpr. Griffiths	Tpr. Grant

" B " SQUADRON ECHELON

Capt. W. R. Hern

S.S.M. Humston	Cpl. Graham
S.Q.M.S. Burke	Cpl. Lowry
Sjt. Fleming	Cpl. McKenzie
Cpl. Nelson	L/Cpl. Gaston
Cpl. Crealey	L/Cpl. Duckers

" B " SQUADRON ECHELON—Continued.

L/Cpl. Miller
L/Cpl. Dunlop
Tpr. Vance
Tpr. McIlveen
Tpr. Hassard
Tpr. Greenfield
Tpr. White, J. A.
Tpr. Fell
Tpr. Wilson
Tpr. Fletcher
Tpr. Mollan
Tpr. Bourne

Tpr. Clarke
Tpr. Robinson
Tpr. Thompson
Tpr. Pilsworth
Tpr. Saunderson
Tpr. Higgins
Tpr. Allen
Tpr. Cantillon
Tpr. White, J.
Tpr. Moffatt
Tpr. Ceirans
Tpr. Waterson

FITTERS
Cpl. Baillie
Tpr. Andrews
Tpr. Coghlan

COOKS
Cpl. Stevenson
Pte. Jameson
Pte. Murray
Pte. Spiers

" C " SQUADRON

H.Q. TROOP	No. 1 TROOP	No. 2 TROOP
Major Morton, M.C.	Lieut. Cumming	L/Sjt. Shaw
Cpl. Yule	L/Cpl. Gregson	Tpr. Lodge
Cpl. Sloan	Tpr. McAloon	Tpr. Lowe
Sjt. Stevenson	L/Cpl. Walker	Tpr. Rodgers
Tpr. Gault	Tpr. Warrender	Tpr. Nolan
Sjt. Christie	Sjt. Garrigan, M.M.	L/Cpl. Boyd
Tpr. Rankin	Tpr. Williams,	Tpr. Ellis
Tpr. McNeill	Tpr. Cockerill	Tpr. Smithdale
L/Cpl. Cowan	Tpr. Neilson, M.M.	Tpr. James
Tpr. Heels	Tpr. Taylor, L.	Tpr. Sibley
Cpl. Owens	L/Sjt. Coxhill	
L/Cpl. Hinxman	Tpr. McGrath	Tpr. Harvey
L/Cpl. Neely	Tpr. Robertson, A.	Tpr. Evans, R.
Tpr. Bigg	L/Cpl. Winyard	L/Cpl. Neill
Tpr. Cooper	Tpr. Millson	

No. 3 TROOP	No. 4 TROOP
Lieut. D. R. King	Lieut. Bexon
L/Cpl. Peters	Trp. Harper, R.
Tpr. Bateson	Tpr. Griffin
Tpr. Gray, E.	Tpr. Gore, B.
L/Sjt. Newell	Sjt. Baker
L/Cpl. Pollard	Tpr. Morrison
Tpr. Lambie	Tpr. Wardle
Tpr. Richardson	L/Cpl. Jefferson
Tpr. Holmes	Tpr. Burton, S.
Cpl. Beal	
Cpl. Ackroyd	
Tpr. Foit	Tpr. Quinn
Tpr. Derbyshire	Tpr. Parfitt
Tpr. McCrea	Tpr. Hewwawell
	Tpr. Cooper

DUG-IN SHERMANS

Capt. F. A. Norris
Cpl. Yule
Sjt. Stevenson
L/Cpl. Green
Tpr. Rankin
Tpr. Neilson, M.M.
Tpr. Williams, P.
Tpr. Lomax
Tpr. Sibley
Tpr. Rodgers
Tpr. Evans
Tpr. Lowe
Tpr. Lodge
Tpr. Bateson
Tpr. McCrea
Tpr. Lambie
Tpr. Leech

Lieut. Hohnen
L/Sjt. Coxhill
Cpl. Gilpin
L/Cpl. Walker
L/Cpl. Gregson
L/Cpl. Winyard
Tpr. McGrath
Tpr. Eastwood
Tpr. McAloon
Tpr. Taylor, L.
Tpr. Robertson
Tpr. Millson
Tpr. Derbyshire
Tpr. Gray, E.
Tpr. Cooper
Tpr. Harper
Tpr. Wardle
Tpr. Quinn

Lieut. Hubbard
Sjt. Baker
L/Sjt. Newell
Cpl. Ackroyd
L/Cpl. Pollard
L/Cpl. Hinxman
L/Cpl. Peters
L/Cpl. James
L/Cpl. Boyd
Tpr. Harvey
Tpr. Harrison, P.
Tpr. Ellis
Tpr. Fort
Tpr. Aldridge, K.
Tpr. Parfitt
Tpr. Burton
Tpr. Morrison

" C " SQUADRON ECHELON

FITTERS

S/Sjt. Williams
  (R.E.M.E.)
Cpl. Mogey
L/Cpl. Green
Tpr. McBay
Cfn. Skilleter
  (R.E.M.E.)

L/Sjt. Stewart
L/Cpl. Dougall
Tpr. Maycock
Tpr. Martin
Tpr. McNeill

SUPPLIES

S.S.M. Bumstead
Sjt. Murray
L/Cpl. Harper
L/Cpl. Dixon
Tpr. Hamilton
Tpr. L'Clery
Tpr. Chartres
Tpr. Bishop
Tpr. McNeill
Tpr. Taylor
Tpr. Jones
Tpr. Stirling
Tpr. Scott (Jeep)

INFANTRY & GUARDS

Cpl. McLernon
L/Cpl. Dixon
L/Cpl. Grindley
Tpr. Jones
Tpr. Devlin
Tpr. Small
Tpr. McNeill
Tpr. Lomax
Tpr. Darragh
Tpr. Taylor, K.
Tpr. Appleyard

H.Q. SQUADRON

Tank and Scout Car Crews

Lieut. G. Mahon

Sjt. Phillips
Sjt. Lytle
Cpl. Lester
L/Cpl. Duke
L/Cpl. Taylor, F.
L/Cpl. Brown, J.
Tpr. Goulburn
Tpr. Robinson, S.
Tpr. Beveridge
Tpr. Critchley
Tpr. Norcliffe
Tpr. Mooney
Tpr. Andrewan
Tpr. Anderson, C.
Tpr. Wilson, J.

Sjt. Sykes
L/Cpl. Casey
L/Cpl. McDougall
L/Cpl. Greenwood
Tpr. Steel
Tpr. Hazelton
Tpr. Cooper
Tpr. Miller
Tpr. Taylor
Tpr. Mason
Tpr. Burrows
Tpr. Houlton
Tpr. Morris

Fitters
Cpl. Johnson, A.
Tpr. Fuller
Tpr. Murphy
Tpr. Andrews

Tpr. Day

Lt. R. G. Whittington

Cpl. Greene
L/Cpl. Simpson
L/Cpl. Shillito
Tpr. Creedon
Tpr. Campbell, S.
Tpr. Mavitty

Tpr. Bitchenor

Sjt. Perioli
Sjt. Wingfield
Cpl. Patterson
Cpl. Brown, H.
L/Cpl. Hadley
L/Cpl. Cannell
Tpr. Bane
Tpr. Dawson, L.
Tpr. Whitehurst
Tpr. Field
Tpr. Harrison, S.
Tpr. Small, S.
Tpr. McCann
Tpr. Smith
Tpr. Creighton
Tpr. McGrath
Tpr. Taylor
Tpr. Snowdon

Sjt. Smyth
Cpl. Marsh, A.
Cpl. Rogers
Cpl. Beal
Tpr. Bibby
Tpr. Phillips
Tpr. Anderson, F.
Tpr. Prince
Tpr. Catton
Tpr. Fisher
Tpr. Humphries
Tpr. Rowbotham
Tpr. Owen
Tpr. Allen

H.Q. SQUADRON ECHELON

Major W. G. Lavery

Capt. E. S. Robinson

R.S.M. Fidler
R.Q.M.S. Docksey
S.S.M. Fowler
Sjt. McWilliams
Sjt. Moorhead
Sjt. McGahey
Sjt. McDonagh
Cpl. Cawley
Cpl. Dunlop
Cpl. Pollitt
Cpl. Rocke, S.
Cpl. Stewart, D.
L/Cpl. Cassidy
L/Cpl. Henderson
L/Cpl. Sutherland
L/Cpl. Garner
L/Cpl. Bogle
L/Cpl. Wolstenholme
L/Cpl. Brownlee, J.
L/Cpl. Dermott
L/Cpl. Moore, R.
Tpr. Armstrong, K.
Tpr. Atkinson
Tpr. Andrew
Tpr. Brookes
Tpr. Bott
Tpr. Brenan
Tpr. Copp
Tpr. Dann

Tpr. Donaghy
Tpr. Ferguson
Tpr. Furphy
Tpr. Fiddes
Tpr. Graham
Tpr. Gray
Tpr. Hanna, D.
Tpr. Hawkins
Tpr. Johnson
Tpr. Kennewell
Tpr. Laverty
Tpr. Latimer
Tpr. Lennon
Tpr. Magee
Tpr. McDowell, W.
Tpr. McDonald, D.
Tpr. Morton
Tpr. McDowell, J.
Tpr. Morris
Tpr. Purvis
Tpr. Reynolds
Tpr. Robertson
Tpr. Shipton
Tpr. Smalley
Tpr. Thompson
Tpr. Vennard
Tpr. Goddenn
Tpr. Young
Tpr. Knopp
Tpr. Broadhurst
Tpr. Moonan

Q.M.S. (M.) Vanstone,
    C.
Sjt. Whyte, A.
Tpr. Dunn
Tpr. Dickenson

Q.M.S. (T.) Scott,   E.
Sjt. Smith, R.A.D.
Cpl. Abbott
L/Cpl. Abbott
L/Cpl. Reid
Tpr. Allard
Tpr. Smith, W.

COOKS
Cpl. McKee
Pte. Evans
Pte. Hitchcock
Pte. Crothers
Tpr. McWilliams

Tpr. Fuller, C.

Tpr. Hart

THE WINTER LINE:

DECEMBER, 1944—APRIL, 1945.

4th December to 11th January—The regiment was in rest at Riccione.

On the 4th December N.I.H. left 25th Army Tank Brigade, which was broken up as a Tank Brigade and reformed as an Assault Engineer Brigade, and joined the 21st Army Tank Brigade in place of the 145th Regiment R.A.C. which had been disbanded. 21st Tank Brigade was commanded by Brigadier D. Dawnay, D.S.O., and the Brigade Second-in-Command was Colonel R. Hamilton-Russell, D.S.O. The other tank regiments in it were the 12th Battalion R. Tanks and the 48th Battalion R. Tanks.

After the usual difficulties the regiment settled down very comfortably in good billets. Leave parties to Rome soon started. Sports, cinemas and clubs helped to entertain us. The Kings' Dragoon Guards gave us ten horses when they went to Greece.

The regiment had great Christmas and New Year celebrations.

12th January, 1945—The regiment moved up to Ravenna and were put in support of the Italian Cremona Gruppo, and C squadron took over from the New Brunswick Hussars in support of an Italian Brigade, from Route 16 to the river Reno.

13th January—A squadron took over from the Governor General's Horse Guards. They had to support an Italian Brigade holding from the sea to the river Senio in what was thought to be a quiet sector. B squadron, regimental headquarters and headquarters squadron were in Ravenna.

14th January to 24th January—The first few days were very trying for the troops in the line. The Italian Infantry were not fully trained and were very excitable. Alarms went on all night, with small arms fire. The Germans re-acted by sending in strong patrols all along the line. These had to be driven out by us next morning.

On the 17th January, Lieut. W. A. L. Reid had a stiff fight, in which he was slightly wounded, to eject the Germans from an Italian position they had captured. He eventually succeeded and restored a very unpleasant position. For this action he won the Military Cross. Italian Infantry were not very reliable so the squadrons made up protective troops from their own echelons to help guard the tanks at night and hold the line. It at last became apparent to all that the Italian Cremona Gruppo had not enough men or sufficient experience to hold so much line so the 2nd Canadian Infantry Brigade came back and took over from Route 16 to the Canale Bonificio. From then on the situation improved.

25th January—The reconnaissance squadron took over A squadron's responsibilities on the coast. The squadron comprised three 95 mm. Churchills, three Shermans, three Honeys and a Command Churchill. Later on it was increased by another Churchill 6-pdr.

troop, made up of the fourth tank of headquarters troop from the other three squadrons. This, in fact, gave the regiment a fourth squadron for static warfare only.

26th January—C squadron, with the Canadians, was relieved by B squadron.

27th January to 3rd February—The Canadians launched a series of small attacks to retake outposts lost by the Italians. B squadron supported these by fire. On the 3rd February a Canadian Platoon was caught by a booby trapped house which blew up, causing them thirty casualties.

This virtually finished all offensive action on this sector.

4th-5th February—All was quiet. Lieut. Maguire stepped on a " S " mine and was lucky to escape with comparatively minor injuries.

6th February—A strong German patrol attacked the Italians on the coast. The Honey Troop, after a harrowing night, restored the situation at daybreak. The Italians had much improved but were not steady when attacked at night. The regiment knew the form by now and took no notice when told the entire German Army was assaulting the Italian platoon, but it was always difficult for the troop on the spot as they never had any idea what was happening till they found out for themselves.

7th-11th February—There was nothing to report during these five days.

12th February—C squadron took over eleven Shermans left by the Canadians in anti-tank roles from Route 16 to the Canale Bonificio. They were supposed to be " dug in " but only one was. They were all badly sited and of little or no use. They had crews of three and these crews were used to thicken up the infantry posts, since the tanks were of no use.

13th-21st February—Routine on all fronts. C squadron was relieved from the " dug in " Shermans.

22nd February—The 17th Infantry Brigade relieved the 2nd Canadian Brigade in B squadron's sector. The 12th Lancers (dismounted) and 2nd Commandos relieved the 22nd Regiment (Italian) astride the Canale Bonificio.

23rd February—The infantry take-over was completed and the regiment remained in the same positions.

24th February—C squadron took over from A squadron and the reconnaissance squadron along the river Reno.

25th-28th February—Nothing to report during this period.

1st March—Plans were finally made for an attack by Italian infantry supported by C squadron (or *vice versa* as it turned out), to clear the base of the " Spit." i.e., the strip of land between Lake Comacchio and the Adriatic Sea.

2nd March—At H hour aircraft were to strafe and bomb the river bank and the point north of Casa Venti, and a " cab rank " was to be available for two hours afterwards. Artillery concentration on Casa Venti and counter-battery fire were to be used during the operation.

The 9th company, 21st Regiment, were to do the initial assault followed by 11th company, 22nd Regiment, and 1st company, 22nd Regiment. No. 3 troop, C squadron, on the right were to move with one platoon of 11th company : No. 2 troop on the left in the woods, and one flame thrower was to go with each troop. H hour was fixed for 1200 hours.

Accompanied by air strafing and artillery concentrations the leading company left Casa Sanze Nome at H hour and reached a position two hundred yards north of Fillopine before making contact. No. 3 troop on the right advanced up the beach carrying their platoon. They dismounted them short of Fillopine and were met by Major Dawson who gave them the picture.

No. 2 troop moved up with a platoon of the reserve company and advanced to a forward position covering Casa Venti. No. 4 troop by this time were in forward positions covering the canal bank. Meanwhile the flame throwers were ordered to pressure up and find a position near Fillopine in readiness for the assault on Casa Venti. The 95 mm. Churchills were given targets to shell in that area.

Just level with Fillopine one flame-thrower blew up on a mine and the other joined No. 3 troop on the beach. No. 3 troop advanced some five hundred yards up the beach and found excellent positions to fire on buildings around Casa Venti. Meanwhile the infantry were held up by a minefield and their sappers were experiencing difficulty in clearing it due to mortar and machine-gun fire. No. 3 troop and the flame-thrower were then ordered to return and close in on Venti, but when coming off the beach two tanks and the flame-thrower blew up on mines. The Royal Engineer troop was brought up to clear this but shelling increased with movement and it became impossible. Sjt. F. Kennedy, M.M., reported enemy troops moving up the beach towards the tanks and all three tanks were engaged with high explosive shells and machine-gun fire, causing casualties, and the enemy withdrew.

During this time aircraft gave excellent close support, sometimes strafing within two hundred yards of our leading troops.

Due to the infantry being held up on the minefield and tanks blowing up, it was decided to consolidate on the present line north of Fillopine. By 1730 hours the two flame throwers and one tank of No. 3 troop were repaired and the troops returned to Borsetti for the night.

3rd March—A further plan was made and H hour fixed at 1115 hours, this time with less air support.

No. 3 troop moved over the ridge of the wood while No. 2 troop moved up to their previous position on the left. No. 3 troop contacted the infantry just clear of Fillopine and were pointed out targets by Major Dawson on their right, consisting of three enemy pillboxes. These they shot up with very good results, and some forty-five to fifty prisoners emerged.

Meantime, on the left, No. 2 troop, after contacting their infantry, moved up into their positions and shot up places around Casa Venti while the infantry moved up to the assault. As soon as they stopped firing the infantry went in and some sixty to seventy prisoners were taken. Six enemy, attempting to get away over the river Reno, were shot at, two believed killed and four taken prisoner.

Shortly after this the squadron leader's tank blew up on a mine near Fillopine and the armoured recovery vehicle plus R.Es. were called forward. The track was swept and the tank repaired within an hour.

The infantry were slowly clearing up the building around Venti and some two hundred prisoners, mostly consisting of Turcomen and Mongolians, had been taken. There were one or two places still occupied by the enemy, but with the assistance of smoke No. 3 troop with their infantry took these and several enemy were killed and wounded, and the remainder taken prisoner. No. 2 troop observed a boat coming round the bend of the river and with their third shot sunk it. At 1700 hours No. 3 troop was ordered to return to harbour. Shortly afterwards No. 2 troop also returned. By this time the infantry had cleared the buildings and consolidated their positions.

4th March—The Jewish Brigade took over a sector of the line south of Route 16. A squadron took over part of the 2nd Armoured Brigade's commitments in support of this Jewish Brigade. These Jews were recruited in Palestine and could mostly speak English. They were very keen and although this was their first experience of fighting they settled down remarkably quickly and were very easy to work with.

The regiment was now in support of fifteen miles of the front. The counter-attack which had been expected earlier in the winter had not materialised and was not likely to do so. The tanks were largely for moral support and for direct shooting so far as the limited allowance of ammunition would permit.

5th March—The 2nd Commando Brigade and 12th Lancers relieved 17th Infantry Brigade on B squadron's sector. The Commandos' original sector astride the Canale Bonificio was taken over by the 1st-11th Battalion of the Cremona Gruppo.

6th March—Sjt. Baker, Troopers Harper, Leech and Quinn were wounded when a shell hit their house.

7th March—The reconnaissance squadron relieved B squadron. A squadron 95 mm. Churchill scored a direct hit on an enemy ammunition dump.

8th-10th March—Nothing to report.

11th March—The reconnaissance squadron took over from C squadron. No tanks were left between Route 16 and the Canale Bonificio but A squadron were made responsible for that area should tanks be required there.

12th-13th March—Further changes in the front were made. This constant changing of infantry formations was partly due to re-organisation for the coming spring offensive and partly to mislead the enemy. The line-up now was :

> South of Route 16 : The Jewish Brigade ⎫ Supported by
> Mezzano to Canale Bonificio : Cremona ⎬ A squadron.
>   Gruppo. ⎭

San Alberto to Lake Commacchio : 12th Lancers and Partisans. ⎤
The " Spit " : 2nd Commando Brigade ⎦ Supported by reconnaissance squadron.

14th-16th March—No change in the positions.

17th March—Saint Patrick's Day was celebrated. The Germans, fortunately, took no part and remained very quiet.

18th March—The Jewish Brigade planned a feint attack for the 20th and after a tussle with Corps our part was satisfactorily arranged.

19th March—A squadron carried out reconnaissance for the attack.

20th March—The Jews sent out strong patrols at 1000 hours, covered by No. 4 troop of A squadron. Two enemy-occupied houses were captured and eight prisoners taken—very valuable for identification at this stage.

21st March—The 2nd Commando Brigade plan for the coming attack on the " Spit " was given to the commanding officer. B squadron were chosen to support them.

22nd March—B squadron started training with the 43rd Commandos for this operation. German patrols during the night attacked 12th Lancers positions covering Alberto and the reconnaissance squadron fired a direct fire programme in for the Lancers.

The regiment had now supported the following " mixed bag " at various times throughout the winter :—

1st Canadian Infantry Brigade.
2nd Canadian Infantry Brigade.
3rd Canadian Infantry Brigade.
Cremona Gruppo (all six Battalions).
2nd Commando Brigade.
12th Royal Lancers.
Jewish Brigade.
17th Indian Infantry Brigade.
Partiganis (Garibaldi Brigade).

25th March—C squadron moved to an area south-west of Ravenna to start training with 19th Indian Infantry Brigade. The regiment was to come under command of the 8th Indian Division for the spring offensive. For the first phase the regiment was to be under command of 19th Brigade. Affiliations were as follows :—

A squadron—1st Argyll and Sutherland Highlanders.
B squadron—8th Punjabs, if available (which they were not).
C squadron—3rd-5th Frontier Force Regiment.

The regiment was lucky to remain in tanks throughout the winter. The fighting from January to April was static. Squadrons were in support of various infantry brigades. Our chief role was counter-attack in the event of an enemy attack. Until ammunition restrictions prevented us, the tanks were used as artillery pieces. The troops lived in houses just behind the main defensive positions and except for an occasional sortie or shoot, did not have much to do. Enemy shelling was heavy at first but died away considerably as the winter wore on.

1st-9th April, 1945—B squadron moved from San Alberto to a concentration area with the Italians. They carried out such training as was possible.

A and C squadrons had a much better training area. They trained and practised with their respective infantry, getting to know the officers and explaining our methods. Both squadrons spent many nights practising night marching across country. This had always been held to be impossible by pundits of the Royal Armoured Corps, but it was found quite practical under certain conditions. This training paid a very handsome dividend in the battle. As many officers as possible took flights in the observation aircraft to have a look at the ground over which we were to attack.

Conferences, Order Groups and reconnaissances took place every day. When the time came, a very elaborate plan went off without the slightest hitch. After considerable argument, the regiment was allotted two Churchill bridge layers (a thirty-feet bridge), two Sherdozers, two Arks and two heavy fascine tanks. This was not enough but would have been just adequate had not every formation borrowed and often misused them.

THE LAKE COMACCHIO OPERATION

Lake Comacchio and the spit of land between it and the sea formed the left flank position of the German Army. The lake is very shallow, with deep mud. The Spit is only a few hundred yards wide.

The amphibious attack by the Commandos, which B squadron supported, was the preliminary move for the spring offensive. It had the following objectives :—

To capture the Spit and draw in German reserves.

To mislead the enemy as to the direction and place of the main attack.

If very successful, to continue round the north of the Lake. Briefly, the plan was an amphibious landing by Commandos from the Lake and an assault crossing of the Reno at its mouth. Thus the attack would come in due east and west. It had been reported by naval patrols that the mouth of the Reno was seven feet deep, so B squadron waterproofed two troops to cross with the assault. The Reno proved to be over twelve feet deep : consequently this did not work out. The other two troops were to cross the Reno on rafts to the west of the Spit in an area held by us and they were to attack along a narrow track between the Reno flood bank and the Lake with two platoons of Commandos in support.

2nd April—After a shaky start, due to the Commando assault boats sticking in the mud, the assault went off as planned. Nos. 2 and 4 troops, B squadron, crossed the Reno at night but were unexpedly held up by a dyke. A fascine was put in this after some delay but by 1600 hours forty prisoners had been taken. Our tanks were behind the German positions in the flood bank and firing into them at point blank range. Just before the leading tank reached the Spit itself, it blew up on a mine, blocking the very narrow track. The last enemy pocket in the south-west corner surrendered when fired on by the tanks. The Commandos had a few casualties.

Meanwhile the other two troops of B squadron had done some good shooting across the mouth of the Reno and knocked out several posts. The Commandos captured or killed nearly two thousand of the enemy.

3rd April—The whole squadron crossed the Reno on rafts and followed up the Commandos who had advanced almost to Porto Garibaldi. There the enemy had a strong defensive position. One tank was hit by a shell but was recovered at once.

At last light B squadron were relieved by the 10th Royal Hussars.

SENIO and FINAL PHASE.

REGIMENTAL H.Q. ADMINISTRATIVE GROUP

Lieut.-Colonel A. W. A. Llewellen-Palmer, D.S.O., M.C.,
Commanding Officer.

Major P. Welch, M.C. ..	.. .. Second-in-Command
Capt. M. B. Pope, M.C. ..	.. .. Adjutant
Capt. J. B. Behr ..	.. .. Liaison Officer
Lieut. B. E. S. King, M.C.	.. .. Signals Officer
Lieut. W. A. Ingram ..	.. .. Intelligence Officer

Sjt. Hamilton
Sjt. Irvine
Cpl. Cox
Cpl. Keenan
Cpl. Reaks
Cpl. Murray
L/Cpl. Plenderleith
L/Cpl. McComish
Tpr. Allen
Tpr. Ging
Tpr. Kennedy
Tpr. Lyttle
Tpr. McIlveen
Tpr. O'Regan

Tpr. Smith
Tpr. Turnham
Tpr. Prince
Tpr. Sherer

Tpr. Wray
Tpr. Noble
Tpr. Hamilton, W.
Tpr. Templeton
Tpr. Wylie
Tpr. Broadhurts
Tpr. Gothorp
Pte. Arnold, A.C.C.

MEDICAL GROUP

Captain P. L. Blaxter,
R.A.M.C.
Cpl. Gleghorne
Tpr. Higgins
Tpr. Holden
Tpr. Strong

ORDER OF BATTLE

" A " SQUADRON

H.Q. TROOP	No. 1 TROOP	No. 2 TROOP
Major Griffith, M.C.	Lieut. Mahony	Lieut. Reid, M.C.
Sjt. Mitchell	Tpr. McKinlay	Tpr. Hodson
L/Cpl. Bainbridge	Tpr. Martin, M.M.	Tpr. Hanshaw
Tpr. Patrick	Tpr. Cameron	L/Cpl. Miller
Tpr. Peden	Tpr. Lees	Tpr. McKeague
Forward Observation Officer	Sjt. McIlherene	Sjt. Barbour, M.M.
Tpr. Wills	Tpr. Sartin	L/Cpl. Moore
Tpr. Harding	Tpr. Reay	Tpr. Harrison
L/Cpl. Graham A.	Tpr. Cree	Tpr. Ranger
Tpr. Todd	Tpr. Badger	Tpr. Hines

H.Q. Troop—cont.	No. 1 Troop—cont.	No. 2 Troop—cont.
Lieut. Waters	Cpl. Burry	Cpl. McKee
Tpr. Cumming	Tpr. Tyndall	Tpr. Jacobs
Tpr. Cowan	Tpr. Barr	Tpr. Wesley
L/Cpl. Harris	L/Cpl. Ainsworth	Tpr. Whyte
Tpr. Connor	Tpr. Tobias	Tpr. McNally

Sjt. Young
Tpr. Howard
Tpr. Green
Tpr. Lynas
Tpr. Morris-Francis

No. 3 Troop	No. 4 Troop
Lieut. Maguire, M.M.	Lieut. Acheson
Tpr. Smith	Tpr. Cassells
Tpr. Clarke	Tpr. Rees
Tpr. Young	Tpr. Lang
Tpr. Stokes, A.	Tpr. Stokes, B.
Sjt. Graham	Sjt. Ballard
Cpl. Hutchman	Tpr. Grey
Tpr. Walker	L/Cpl. Robinson
Tpr. Parker	Tpr. Gledhill
Tpr. Sharkey	Tpr. Lymer
Sjt. Craig	Cpl. Watson
Tpr. Donaldson	Tpr. Farmer
Tpr. McConnell	L/Cpl. Conroy
Tpr. McWilliams	Tpr. Mann
Tpr. Taggart	Tpr. Hughes

RELIEFS AND SPARE
CREWS
Sjt. Smith
L/Cpl. Crisp
Tpr. McKinlay
Tpr. Hancher
Tpr. Calland

JEEP
Tpr. Mann
L/Cpl. Graham, D.

SCOUT CAR
Capt. King
Tpr. Bell

VEHICLE MECHANICS' ECHELON

A.R.V. Crew		HALF-TRACK
L/Sjt. Jackson	Sjt. Trotter	S/Sjt. Derrick, R.E.M.E.
Tpr. Bailey	Cpl. Duffin	Tpr. Eyre
Tpr. Gallaher	Tpr. Howat	Tpr. Sherlock
Tpr. Hawkridge	Tpr. Meichen	Tpr. Sullivan
Cfn. Mattick, R.E.M.E.		

" A " SQUADRON ECHELON

Capt. R. H. Bowring

S.S.M. Boon
S.Q.M.S. Allen
Sjt. Moore
Cpl. Baker
Cpl. Haren
Cpl. Lyne
Cpl. Lavery
L/Cpl. Cunningham
L/Cpl. Cox, R.
L/Cpl. McKillen
L.U.L.C. Marshall
L.U.L.C. Patton
Tpr. Armstrong
Tpr. Coyle
Tpr. Cunningham

Tpr. Duncan
Tpr. Eakins
Tpr. Henderson
Tpr. Kane
Tpr. Lissaman
Tpr. Malcolmson
Tpr. Morrison
Tpr. Mitchell
Tpr. McLaughlin
Tpr. McCombe
Tpr. Richmond
Tpr. Reynolds
Tpr. Wells
Tpr. Wesley, H.
Tpr. William, J.
Tpr. Ward

FITTERS
L/Cpl. Lockhart
Tpr. Barnacle
Tpr. Stoker

COOKS
L.U.L.C. Griffiths
Pte. Chartres
Pte. Flynn
Pte. Hales
Pte. Kelly

" B " SQUADRON

H.Q. TROOP	No. 1 TROOP	No. 2 TROOP
Major Sidebottom	Lieut. Moorhead	Lieut. B. Pope
Cpl. Wiggins	Tpr. Johnston	Tpr. Ward
L/Cpl. Hughes	Tpr. Gray	L/Cpl. Martin
Tpr. Beggs	Tpr. Buxton	Tpr. Shanks
Tpr. Johnston, J. B.	Tpr. O'Keefe	Tpr. Knott
Sjt. Wolfe	Sjt. Bullick	Sjt. McAughtry
Tpr. Sharples	Tpr. McKinney	Tpr. Walker
Cpl. Kelville	Tpr. Fuller	Tpr. Kerr
L/Cpl. Collard	Tpr. Robinson, A.	Tpr. Jennings
Tpr. Dawson	Tpr. Moore, H. J.	Tpr. Ibbotson
Lieut. Foott	Cpl. Wheatley	Sjt. Buchanan
Cpl. Walls	Tpr. Coppin	Tpr. Harrow
Tpr. Wood	Tpr. French	Tpr. Rexworthy
Tpr. Dalzell	Tpr. Bishop	Tpr. Cawley
—	Tpr. Bateson	Tpr. Hanson
Sjt. McCullough		
—		
Tpr. Bowers		
Tpr. Young		
—		

No. 4 Troop	No. 5 Troop
Lieut. Mahon	Lieut. Bullick
L/Cpl. Giboney	L/Cpl. Marcham
Tpr. Dawson, R.	L/Cpl. Darville
L./Cpl. Moore	Tpr. Darville
Tpr. Holt	Tpr. Brotton
Sjt. White	Sjt. Smith
Tpr. Fitzgerald	Tpr. White, V. N.
L/Cpl. Fennell	Tpr. Parker
Tpr. Dixon	L/Cpl. Binstead
Tpr. Gamble	Tpr. Gomm
Cpl. Malseed	Sjt. Cheater
Tpr. Webb	Tpr. Gardiner
Tpr. Jeffrey	Tpr. Sumners
Tpr. Perkins	L/Cpl. Wallace
Tpr. Warner	Tpr. Symonds

FORWARD ECHELON

FITTERS	A.R.V. CREW
Sjt. Holmes	L/Cpl. Hughes
Cpl. Day	L/Cpl. Beatty
Tpr. Brindle	Tpr. Handley
L/Cpl. Wallace	Tpr. Gilligan
L/Cpl. Russell	Tpr. Donaghy

SCOUT CAR	JEEP
Tpr. Griffiths	Tpr. Grant, W.

"B" SQUADRON ECHELON

Capt. W. R. Hern

S.S.M. Humston	Tpr. Fell
S.Q.M.S. Burke	Tpr. Wilson
Sjt. Fleming	Tpr. Fletcher
Cpl. Nelson	Tpr. Mollan
Cpl. Crealey	Tpr. Bourne
Cpl. Graham	Tpr. Clarke
Cpl. Lowry	Tpr. Robinson
Cpl. McKenzie	Tpr. Thompson
L/Cpl. Gaston	Tpr. Pilsworth
L/Cpl. Duckers	Tpr. Saunderson
L/Cpl. Miller	Tpr. Higgins
L/Cpl. Dunlop	Tpr. Allen
Tpr. Vance	Tpr. Cantillon
Tpr. McIlveen	Tpr. White, J.
Tpr. Hassard	Tpr. Moffatt
Tpr. Greenfield	Tpr. Ceirans
Tpr. White, J. A.	Tpr. Waterson

FITTERS	COOKS
Cpl. Baillie	Cpl. Stevenson
Tpr. Andrews	Pte. Jameson
Tpr. Coghlan	Pte. Murray
	Pte. Spiers

" C " SQUADRON

H.Q. TROOP	No. 1 TROOP	No. 2 TROOP
Major Morton, M.C.	Lieut. A. N. MacCleary	Lieut. R. A. Hubbard
Cpl. Yule	Tpr. Williams, P.	L/Cpl. Gregson
Cpl. Sloan	Tpr. McAloon	Tpr. Smithdale
Tpr. Heels	Cpl. Gilpin	L/Cpl. James
Tpr. Hellawell	Tpr. Neilson, M.M.	Tpr. Nolan
Capt. Thomas, M.C.		
Capt. Norris		
Capt. Milne	Sjt. Thacker	Sjt. Bell
Cpl. Owens	Tpr. Dyer	Tpr. Ellis
Tpr. Halligan	Tpr. Clegg	Tpr. Lowe
Tpr. Millson	Tpr. Eastwood	Tpr. Evans
Tpr. Allen	Tpr. Cockerill	Tpr. Harvey
		Tpr. Maycock
Sjt. Christie	L/Sjt. Coxhill	L/Sjt. Newell/and Shaw
Tpr. Tankin	Tpr. McGrath	Tpr. Lodge
Tpr. McNeill	Tpr. Robertson	Tpr. Armstrong
L/Cpl. Cowan	L/Cpl. Winyard	Tpr. Rodgers
Tpr. Gault, W.	Tpr. Warrender	Tpr. Sibley
L/Sjt. Newell		
Tpr. Warnock		
Tpr. Ledger		
Tpr. Bigg		
Tpr. Cooper		
Cpl. Owens		
L/Cpl. Neely		

No. 3 TROOP	No. 4 TROOP
Lieut. D. R. King	Lieut. M. L. Bexon
L/Cpl. Peters	L/Cpl. Green
Tpr. Bateson	Tpr. Griffin
Tpr. Gray, E.	Cpl. Hamilton
Tpr. Holmes	Tpr. Maycock
Sjt. Kennedy, M.M.	Sjt. Brocklehurst, M.M.
Tpr. Aldridge	Tpr. Moles
Tpr. Fort	Tpr. Parfitt
Tpr. Derbyshire	L/Cpl. Walker
Tpr. McCrea	Tpr. Tattersall
Cpl. Ackroyd	L/Sjt. Williams, F. B.
L/Cpl. Pollard	Tpr. Morrison
Tpr. Lambie	Tpr. Wardle
Tpr. Richardson	L/Cpl. Jefferson
	Tpr. Harrison, P.

FITTERS

Sjt. Gettings	L/Sjt. Stewart, M.M.
Cpl. McAteer	Cpl. Mogey
L/Cpl. Green	L/Cpl. Dougall
Tpr. Thompson	Tpr. Martin
Tpr. Hill	Tpr. Davis
Tpr. McBay	Tpr. McNeill
Cfn. Skilleter, R.E.M.E.	

98

" C " SQUADRON ECHELON

S.S.M. Bumstead
Cpl. McLernon
Tpr. Bishop
Tpr. O'Clery
Tpr. Spellman
Tpr. Appleyard
Tpr. Stirling (Scout Car)

Sjt. Murray
L/Cpl. Dixon
Tpr. Hamilton
Tpr. Chartres
Tpr. Small
Tpr. Scott (Jeep)

H.Q. SQUADRON

TANK AND SCOUT CAR CREWS

Lt. R. G. Whittington   Lieut. G. Mahon

Cpl. Greene
L/Cpl. Simpson
L/Cpl. Shillito
Tpr. Creedon
Tpr. Campbell, S.

Tpr. Bitchenor

Sjt. Sykes
L/Cpl. Casey
L/Cpl. McDougall
L/Cpl. Greenwood
Tpr. Steel
Tpr. Hazelton
Tpr. Cooper
Tpr. Miller
Tpr. Taylor
Tpr. Mason
Tpr. Burrows
Tpr. Houlton
Tpr. Morris

Sjt. Smyth
Cpl. Marsh
Cpl. Rogers
Cpl. Beal
Tpr. Bibby
Tpr. Phillips
Tpr. Chapman
Tpr. Anderson
Tpr. Prince
Tpr. Catton
Tpr. Fisher

FITTERS
Cpl. Johnson, A.
Tpr. Fuller
Tpr. Murphy
Tpr. Andrew
Tpr. Porter

Sjt. Phillips
Sjt. Lytle
Cpl. Lester
L/Cpl. Brown, J.
L/Cpl. Taylor, F.
Tpr. Goulburn
Tpr. Robinson
Tpr. Beveridge
Tpr. Citichley
Tpr. Norcliffe
Tpr. Mooney
Tpr. Andrewan
Tpr. Anderson, C.
Tpr. Lang

Sjt. Perioli, S.
Sjt. Wingfield
Cpl. Brown, H.
Cpl. Illingworth
L/Cpl. Hadley
L/Cpl. Cannell
Tpr. Bane
Tpr. Dawson, R.
Tpr. Whitehurst
Tpr. Field
Tpr. Harrison
Tpr. Small, S.
Tpr. McCann
Tpr. Smith
Tpr. Creighton
Tpr. McGrath

Tpr. Humphries
Tpr. Rowbotham
Tpr. Owen
Tpr. Askew
Tpr. Allen

Tpr. Day

H.Q. SQUADRON ECHELON

Major W. G. Lavery   Capt. E. S. Robinson

R.S.M. Fidler
R.Q.M.S. Docksey
S.S.M. Fowler
Sjt. McWilliams
Sjt. Moorhead
Sjt. McCahey
Sjt. McDonagh
Cpl. Cawley
Cpl. Dunlop
Cpl. Pollitt
Cpl. Rocke, S.
Cpl. Stewart, D.
L/Cpl. Cassidy
L/Cpl. Henderson
L/Cpl. Sutherland
L/Cpl. Garner
L/Cpl. Bogle
L/Cpl. Wolstenholme
L/Cpl. Dermott
L/Cpl. Moore, R.
L/Cpl. Neely
Tpr. Armstrong
Tpr. Atkinson
Tpr. Andrew
Tpr. Brookes
Tpr. Bott
Tpr. Brenan
Tpr. Copp
Tpr. Dann

Tpr. Donaghy
Tpr. Ferguson
Tpr. Furphy
Tpr. Fiddes
Tpr. Gray
Tpr. Hanna, D.
Tpr. Hawkins
Tpr. Johnson
Tpr. Kennewell
Tpr. Laverty
Tpr. Logue
Tpr. Latimer
Tpr. Lennon
Tpr. Magee
Tpr. McDowell, W.
Tpr. McDonnell, D.
Tpr. Morton
Tpr. McDowell, J.
Tpr. Morris
Tpr. Purvis
Tpr. Reynolds
Tpr. Robertson
Tpr. Shipton
Tpr. Smalley
Tpr. Thompson
Tpr. Vennard
Tpr. Young
Tpr. Knopp
Tpr. Moonan

Q.M.S. (M.) Vanstone,
  C.
Sjt. Whyte, A.
Tpr. Dunn
Tpr. Dickenson

Q.M.S. (T.) Scott, F.
Sjt. Smith, R.A.D.
Cpl. Abbott
L/Cpl. Abbott
L/Cpl. Reid
Tpr. Allard
Tpr. Smith, W.

COOKS
Cpl. McKee
Pte. Evans
Pte. Hitchcock
Pte. Crothers
Tpr. McWilliams

Sjt. Walford
Tpr. Fuller, C.

Tpr. Hart
Tpr. Chapman, G.

RIVER SENIO ASSAULT.

FINAL PHASE.

The enemy had his main defensive positions between the Senio and Santerno rivers, inclusive.

The Army plan was to break this line by frontal assault, then to swing north through the Argenta Gap, and destroy the enemy south of the River Po.

A and C squadrons were under command of the 19th Indian Infantry Brigade—B squadron were in support of the Cremona Gruppo, who were to attempt a crossing north of Fusignano if the other crossings proved successful. The 8th Indian Division and the New Zealand Division were the assaulting Divisions north of Route 16. The 8th Indian Divisional area was between Lugo and Fusignano, of which 17th Indian Infantry Brigade and the N.I.H. had the north : 21st Indian Infantry Brigade and the 48th Battalion R. Tanks had the south.

9th April—Throughout the day heavy bombing and shelling programmes were carried out. In the evening the tanks and flame throwers went right up to the Senio flood banks and opened fire. The infantry assaulted through the tanks and captured both banks without much difficulty.

10th April—A Bailey bridge was in position by 0330 hours and tanks of A and C squadrons crossed without incident. They were met on the far side by guides from the regiment who had crossed with the assaulting infantry and the troops were shown the way to the various infantry companies. Capt. J. S. Milne was C squadron's guide. For this and some exceptionally good reconnaissance work in the advance to the Santerno he was awarded the Military Cross. Every troop was in its proper position and moving forward with its infantry before first light : A squadron on the right with the Argyll and Sutherland Highlanders ; C squadron on the left with the Frontier Force Regiment. C squadron crossed the Arginello Canal and were faced by the Tratturo Canal which had been prepared as an anti-tank defensive zone—all trees felled, houses blown down, mines laid and anti-tank guns positioned. Nos. 3 and 4 troops halted on the Lugo Canal and engaged the enemy. They knocked out one enemy self-propelled anti-tank gun but could not cross the open in daylight.

Lieut. Bexon removed the charges from the Arginello Canal in full view of the enemy, thus saving several hours of vital time He also knocked out one of the self-propelled guns and led the advance to the Tratturo. For this he was awarded the Military Cross.

The Frontier Force Regiment were very tired so the brigadier decided to pass the Punjab Regiment through them at night, the tanks to make their own crossings with Arks and fascines ; C squadron and the Punjabs then to attack and reach the Santerno.

101

This was successfully accompished without much fighting as the enemy had pulled out with his heavy equipment, leaving only light machine-guns.

Meanwhile A squadron, with Nos. 1 and 4 Troops leading, found a crossing of the Lugo Canal and formed a small bridgehead over it with the infantry. At 0800 hours Nos. 1 and 2 troops set off by themselves to reconnoitre north west and exploit, if possible. They made considerable progress but were eventually held up by a self-propelled gun. This gun was engaged and withdrew. A dismounted troop of the 6th Lancers then came up and joined No. 1 troop. Together they reached the Arginello. They engaged enemy positions and a tank, and reconnoitred for a crossing.

B squadron, with the Italians who had made a successful crossing, were unable to cross owing to bridging difficulties. Two troops were ordered to cross on the 19th Infantry Brigade Bailey bridge. This they did but were unable to join the Italians west of the Senio owing to canals and blown bridges. B squadron suffered throughout this operation from a lack of Engineer Assault Bridging equipment. The Italian attack was planned only at the last minute and was in the nature of a side show. These two troops had to go back over 19th Brigade bridge and eventually crossed by the long awaited Italian Bailey bridge.

11th April—C squadron were relieved by a Sherman squadron of the 4th Hussars under command of the N.I.H. This squadron led an attack north between the rivers Senio and Santerno. They made good progress for two thousand yards when they ran into an anti-tank gun which knocked out the leading Sherman, killing four of the crew. C squadron joined up with 21st Indian Infantry Brigade who had come up on our left.

The 4th Hussars were withdrawn in the afternoon and rejoined their own regiment.

A squadron had a quiet day preparing for a night advance.

B squadron managed to get two troops and squadron headquarters over the river by 0100 hours—the remainder got over in the course of the day. Nos. 2 and 5 troops joined the Italians and cut Route 16 while the Italians entered Alfonsine. Major Sidebottom had great difficulty in getting any plans or information out of the Italians—the three Generals who commanded this Brigade were in hot dispute amongst themselves, but in spite of their commanders the Italian soldiers did very well.

Night of 11th-12th April—A squadron accomplished a most spectacular night march—unaccompanied by infantry they crossed six thousand yards of difficult country using their own bridging devices By dawn they had reached the Santerno, three miles north of C squadron. Unfortunately the enemy had just pulled out and by a few minutes had escaped the trap.

At 0800 hours three troops reached the Senio-Reno river junction, thus clearing all the country in front of the Italians. The Santerno proved to be strongly held and all bridges gone. A squadron were recalled to avoid misunderstandings with the Italians who now had a clear run to the river Santerno.

C squadron moved north and joined up with A squadron, capturing a few stragglers on the way.

B squadron came along Route 16 as fast as bridging permitted and contacted A squadron patrols by last light.

13th April—The 19th Indian Infantry Brigade was withdrawn for a well-earned rest so A and C squadrons had a rest. Major R. D. Morton, M.C., had a badly swollen knee and had to go back ; Capt. C. M. Thomas, M.C., took over C squadron.

B squadron were ordered to give all possible support to the Italians who planned an assault crossing of the Santerno.

At 0630 hours No. 5 troop advanced straight up Route 16. Lieut. B. L. Pope got his tank on top of the flood bank and opened fire on the far bank. The tank was hit by a Panzerfaust but was not penetrated. They reversed out over several mines that did not go off. The Italian infantry was pinned down by mortar and Spandau fire and never reached the bank.

Meanwhile No. 4 troop went forward without the infantry who were not ready. They entered La Pastorello without opposition and, advancing through thick vines, reached the Santerno by a blown railway bridge. They shot up all enemy posts they could observe. They were heavily mortared. At mid-day the troop collected the Italian Infantry and again attacked the bank, this time driving right up to it. This attack failed. At 1600 hours they attacked again and on this occasion the Italians went across. Lieut. K. W. Foott did very excellent work rallying and leading the Italians on his feet. He was awarded the Military Cross. There were no Italian officers present.

14th April—A tank crossing had been made during the night, but B squadron were no longer required as the 2nd Armoured Brigade had already reached the Argenta bridge from the south. The total number of prisoners was two hundred and fifty in this action—the dead were not counted. B squadron came under command of the regiment again and settled down in La Pastorella.

15th-19th April—The regiment was in Army reserve with the 8th Indian Division. This was a very fortunate break for us and a very unusual one. It allowed everyone to get some sleep and the tanks to be fully maintained. The remarkable achievement of having every tank in the regiment still going when the Campaign ended was due to first-class recovery and repair work by the regimental fitters and the light aid detachment. No other tank regiment has ever achieved this, even with Shermans. Churchill tanks are by far the most difficult to keep on the road.

20th April—The regiment, ordered to support 8th Indian Division up Route 16 and to capture Ferrara, moved to a concentration area near Consondola.

21st April—B squadron with the 17th Indian Infantry Brigade moved up Route 16 meeting only light opposition.

22nd April—B squadron with the Punjabs continued the advance. When within two miles of Ferrara the opposition stiffened. At 1600 hours B squadron with the Argyll and Sutherland Highlanders passed through A squadron and reached the canal south of Ferrara.

The canal bridge was blown up in sight of the leading troop. No assault crossing equipment was immediately available so they had to wait.

Meanwhile C squadron, with the 21st Indian Infantry Brigade, had made a rapid advance north on a parallel road west of Route 16 and reached the south western outskirts of Ferrara where they were held up by several German tanks. At last light these withdrew into the town and blew up the bridge behind them.

23rd April—At first light Nos. 3 and 4 troops of C squadron, commanded by Capt Milne, were ordered to advance to the River Po, and prevent the enemy from using some known ferrying place. By 1045 hours No. 3 Troop (Lieut. D. R. King) reached the Po and captured a large assortment of vehicles, stores, etc. This virtually cut off the strong German force holding Ferrara. For this and for previous excellent work Lieut. King was awarded the Military Cross.

Nos. 1 and 2 troops under Capt. F. A. Norris supported the 1st Mahratta Regiment in clearing up all the country south of the Po di Volano. They had some stiff fighting but succeeded in their task.

B squadron, with the Jaipurs, fought their way into the factory area on the west of Ferrara. They met with very stiff opposition from German tanks. There was only one possible crossing over the canal running round the town and this was covered by tanks and self-propelled guns hidden in the factories.

As soon as it was dark B squadron crossed and cleaned up the factory area, then drove into the town where they met A squadron who had crossed with the Argyll and Sutherland Highlanders at the south-eastern corner. Lieut. W. A. L. Reid of A squadron killed twenty Germans with one shot as they were forming up, presumably to march away.

Eight German tanks and two self-propelled guns were captured during this night assault. No opposition was met, the enemy being taken completely by surprise.

24th April—The regiment was ordered to prepare to cross the Po on rafts. There was considerable confusion as to who was providing these. The whole Ferrara area was finally cleaned up.

25th April—The regiment moved to concentration areas for crossing and carried out reconnaissance. Plans changed so often that they cannot be recorded.

Rafts finally did arrive and C squadron started to cross. There was no opposition.

26th April—By 1000 hours most of C squadron were over. Two troops of A squadron got across but very heavy rain delayed operations.

27th April—C squadron made a long detour over unblown bridges and arrived two thousand yards short of the River Adige by last light. Here they joined up with the 17th Indian Infantry Brigade. The remainder of the Regiment crossed the Po.

29th April—C squadron caught a very large enemy column of guns, tanks and every sort and kind of vehicle trying to cross the

Adige ; abandoned German equipment was everywhere along the river—even more than there had been along the Po and it was obvious to all that the end would not be long delayed.

And so on the 30th April, 1945, the North Irish Horse was ordered to " Stand Down " for the last time.

The regiment took part in some of the hardest fighting of the Campaign. From the 1st until the 30th April only one officer—Lieut. D. L. Knight, B.E.M.—was slightly wounded Several tanks were hit but not knocked out. This was due to the skill of tank commanders.

Roll of Honour.

KILLED—NORTH AFRICA

MAJOR J. REW

CAPT. D. A. LESLIE, R.E.M.E.	2nd LT. R. P. M. MANN
SQMS. A. S. BROWN	SJT. P. J. WALTERS
SJT. N. HEWITT	CPL. W. MANAMLEY
CPL. R. DIXON	L-CPL. R. S. HAZELDINE
L-CPL. D. F. O'FARRELL	L-CPL. W. JAMESON
TPR. J. NURSEY	TPR. J. FRANKLIN
TPR. L. ISHERWOOD	TPR. A. WHALLEY
TPR. J. H. RYAN	TPR. G. DAVIES
TPR. R. J. CURRIE	TPR. D. McFAUL

L-CPL. N. HUTCHINSON

KILLED—ITALY

LIEUT.-COLONEL THE LORD O'NEILL
MAJOR W. M. MACKEAN, M.C.

LT. G. C. BROWN, M.C.	LIEUT. R. M. HORSBURGH
LIEUT. J. H. PYL	LIEUT. T. G. TUCKEY
SJT. W. J. BEST	SJT. L. REEVE
SJT. A. G. ELLIOTT	SJT. J. McLAUGHLIN
SJT. T. J. McQUEEN	SJT. J. CLULOW
SJT. R. E. BONE	SJT. H. McI. BURNS
CPL. A. J. CANTWELL	CPL. P. ASPREY
L-CPL. S. COX	L-CPL. R. MILLIKEN
L-CPL H. JENKINS	L-CPL. H. PRYDE
L-CPL. J. BENSON	L-CPL. T. S. CHAMBERS
L-CPL. B. L. SQUIRES	L-CPL. A. JACKSON
L-CPL. W. HILL	TPR. U. G. LOVE
TPR. M. S. STRONG	TPR. R. NEWTON
TPR. R. C. ELLIS	TPR. T. PRICE
TPR. W. CURRIE	TPR. J. RUTHERFORD
TPR. N. W. MOSS	TPR. C. J. F. SMITH
TPR. J. A. STEWART	TPR. J. W. WILSON
TPR. A. CODD	TPR. A. E. BATEMAN
TPR. T. DUNNE	TPR. J. GALLOWAY
TPR. A. J CARTMALE	TPR. F. A. DAVAGE
TPR. B. G. COOTE	TPR. J. BRADFIELD
TPR. D. LOXDALE	TPR. J. T. TWEEDIE
TPR. D. G. JAMES	TPR. R. J. MITCHELL
TPR. H. J. BARWELL	TPR. G. KING
TPR. N. CORBIN	TPR. R. A. STAFFORD

TPR. J. WOOD

HONOURS AND AWARDS.

DISTINGUISHED SERVICE ORDER

LIEUT.-COLONEL D. DAWNAY
LIEUT.-COLONEL E. V. STRICKLAND, M.M.

DISTINGUISHED CONDUCT MEDAL

SJT. T. MCAUGHTRY

MEMBER OF THE BRITISH EMPIRE

MAJOR W. W. G. LAVERY
CAPTAIN A. D. WILSON
R.Q.M.S. W. DOCKSEY

MILITARY CROSS

MAJOR G. P. RUSSELL	MAJOR P. WELCH
MAJOR R. D. MORTON	MAJOR R. S. H. SIDEBOTTOM
CAPT. R. J. GRIFFITH	CAPT. W. M. MACKEAN
CAPT. C. M. THOMAS	CAPT. R. B. M. KING
CAPT. A. K. E. FINCH NOYES	CAPT. J. S. MILNE
LIEUT. M. B. POPE	LIEUT. G. C. BROWN
LIEUT. G. E. GARDINER	LIEUT. H. E. IRWIN
LIEUT. B. E. S. KING	LIEUT. W. A. L. REID
LIEUT. K. W. FOOTT	LIEUT. M. L. BEXON

LIEUT. D. R. KING
LIEUT. A. MAGUIRE, M.M.

BAR TO MILITARY CROSS

MAJOR R. J. GRIFFITH, M.C.

MILITARY MEDAL

S.S.M. L. BUMSTEAD	SJT. E. O'HARE
SJT. J. MAXWELL	SJT. J. E. BARBOUR
SJT. T. W. DONAGHY	SJT. F. VERSO
SJT. G. BALLARD	SJT. J. C. BUCHANAN
L/SJT. J. STEWART	CPL. R. B. COX
CPL. W. T. GLEGHORNE	CPL. J. J. CUNNINGHAM
L/CPL. A. MAGUIRE	L/CPL. F. D. KENNEDY
L/CPL. C. M. MORIARTY	L/CPL. F. J. HAM
L/CPL. W. HUGHES	TPR. A. B. CHURCH
TPR. S. JOHNSTON	TPR. J. D. NEILSON
TPR. G. E. MARTIN	

BAR TO MILITARY MEDAL

TPR. J. D. NEILSON, M.M.
TPR. S. JOHNSTON, M.M.

BRITISH EMPIRE MEDAL

SJT. D. L. KNIGHT

HONOURS AND AWARDS—Continued.

AMERICAN SILVER STAR
CAPT. G. MAHON

AMERICAN BRONZE STAR
SJT. F. D. KENNEDY

MENTIONED IN DESPATCHES
LIEUT.-COLONEL THE LORD O'NEILL

Major J. REW
CAPT. J. S. MILNE, M.C.
LIEUT. E. D. BULLICK
LIEUT. K. W. FOOTT, M.C.
S.S.M. L. C. BUMSTEAD
S.S.M. R. W. FOWLER
SJT. T. HAMILTON
SJT. A. G. ELLIOTT
SJT. K. CHEATER
SJT. J. E. BARBOUR
SJT. W. MITCHELL
L/SJT. S. C. JACKSON
L/SJT. J. STEWART, M.M.
CPL. A. G. CHESTER
CPL. R. E. GALE
L/CPL. W. HUGHES
L/CPL. W. WHEATLEY
L/CPL. R. WALLACE
L/CPL. E. RICHARDSON
TPR. T. ROOKE
TPR. A. HUGHES
TPR. J. MARTIN
TPR. J. BROWNLEE
TPR. D. KNOTT
S.Q.M.S. D. BURKE
SJT. V. ILLINGWORTH
SJT. A. JOHNSTON
SJT. W. McGAHEY
L/CPL. F. R. WILSON
TPR. B. GORE

CAPT. J. E. WILLIAMS
CAPT. E. M. HUGHES (Padre)
LIEUT. D. F. HUNT
LIEUT. R. E. PERIOLI
S.S.M. W. DOCKSEY
S.S.M. J. LESLIE
SJT. W. J. BEST
SJT. T. McAUGHTRY, D.C.M.
SJT. T. M. DONAGHY
SJT. D. A. GRAHAM
SJT. W. J. A. WHYTE
SJT. B. BAKER
L/SJT. H. SHAW
CPL. T. CAWLEY
CPL. H. BROWN
CPL. C. HAMILTON
L/CPL. W. J. KEENAN
L/CPL. T. W. MOORE
TPR. W. J. COWAN
TPR. T. J. WHYTE
TPR. H. MILLSON
TPR. G. ATKINSON
TPR. E. HAMILTON
TPR. T. McKEAGUE
S.S.M. J. ALLEN
SJT. R. G. BELL
SJT. T. H. STEVENSON
SJT. T. MOORE
L/SJT. J. LOWRY
TPR. J. DONALDSON
TPR. W. J. McCANN

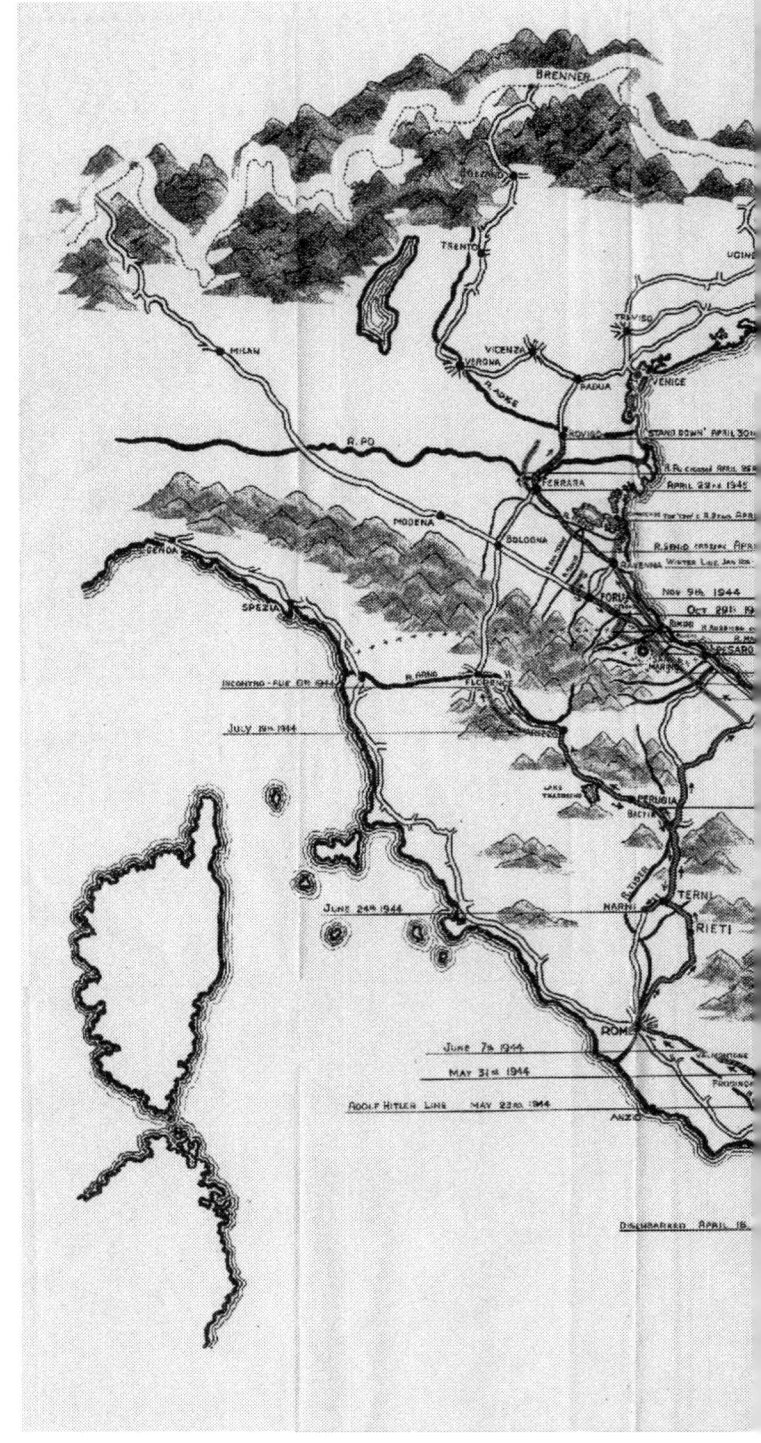

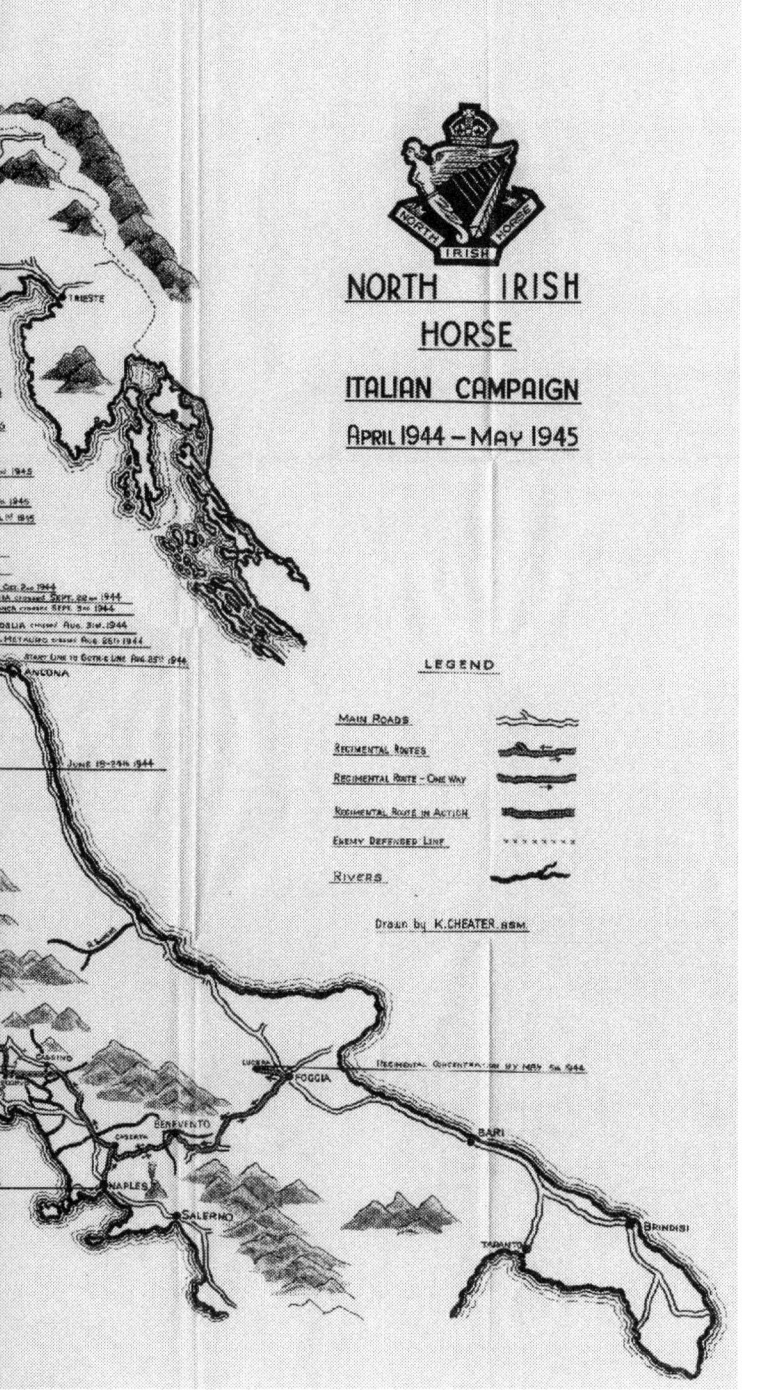

NORTH   IRISH
HORSE
ITALIAN CAMPAIGN
April 1944 – May 1945

LEGEND

Main Roads	
Regimental Routes	
Regimental Route – One Way	
Regimental Route in Action	
Enemy Defended Line	
Rivers	

Drawn by K.CHEATER. BEM.